GOODSON MUMBA

Africa's Financial Horizon

Opportunities and Challenges for Investors

Copyright © 2024 by Goodson Mumba

All rights reserved. No part of this publication may be reproduced, stored or transmitted in any form or by any means, electronic, mechanical, photocopying, recording, scanning, or otherwise without written permission from the publisher. It is illegal to copy this book, post it to a website, or distribute it by any other means without permission.

First edition

ISBN: 9798333734051

This book was professionally typeset on Reedsy. Find out more at reedsy.com

Contents

Preface	vii
Acknowledgments	ix
Dedication	x
Disclaimer	xi
1 Chapter 1: The Decision	1
1.1: Overview of African Economies	1
1.2 Historical Context of Investment in Africa	4
1.3 Current Economic Trends	6
1.4 Key Sectors for Investment	9
1.5 Regional Economic Communities and Trade Blocs	12
1.6 Summary and Conclusion	15
2 Chapter 2: Understanding the Investment Landscape	21
2.1: Investment Types and Vehicles	21
2.2 Regulatory Environment	24
2.3 Legal Frameworks for Investors	26
2.4 Financial Institutions and Market Infrastructure	28
2.5 Key Investment Policies and Reforms	30
2.6 Summary and Conclusion	33
3 Chapter 3: Risk Management in African Investments	35
3.1 Identifying Investment Risks	35
3.2: Political and Economic Risks	37

	3.3: Currency and Exchange Rate Risks	40
	3.4: Social and Cultural Risks	42
	3.5: Strategies for Risk Mitigation	44
	3.6: Summary and Conclusion	47
4	Chapter 4: Sectoral Opportunities in Africa	50
	4.1: Agriculture and Agribusiness	50
	4.2: Energy and Natural Resources	52
	4.3: Technology and Telecommunications	55
	4.4: Infrastructure and Real Estate	57
	4.5: Financial Services	60
	4.6: Healthcare and Pharmaceuticals	62
5	Chapter 5: Investing in Infrastructure	66
	5.1: The Need for Infrastructure Development	66
	5.2: Transportation Networks	68
	5.3: Energy Infrastructure	71
	5.4: Water and Sanitation Projects	73
	5.5: Public-Private Partnerships	76
	5.6: Summary and Conclusion	78
6	Chapter 6: The Role of Technology and Innovation	81
	6.1: Digital Transformation in Africa	81
	6.2: Fintech and Financial Inclusion	84
	6.3: Tech Hubs and Startups	86
	6.4: E-Commerce and Mobile Payments	88
	6.5: Opportunities in ICT Infrastructure	91
	6.6: Summary and Conclusion	93
7	Chapter 7: Agricultural Investment Opportunities	96
	7.1: The Importance of Agriculture in Africa	96
	7.2: Agribusiness Value Chains	98
	7.3: Investment in Agricultural Technology	101
	7.4: Land Ownership and Regulatory Issues	103
	7.5: Sustainable Agricultural Practices	106

	7.6: Summary and Conclusion	108
8	Chapter 8: Energy and Natural Resources	111
	8.1: Overview of Africa's Energy Landscape	111
	8.2: Renewable Energy Opportunities	113
	8.3: Oil and Gas Sector	116
	8.4: Mining and Minerals	118
	8.5: Environmental Considerations	121
	8.6: Summary and Conclusion	123
9	Chapter 9: Real Estate and Urban Development	126
	9.1: Urbanization Trends in Africa	126
	9.2: Residential and Commercial Real Estate	129
	9.3: Affordable Housing Initiatives	132
	9.4: Investment in Smart Cities	134
	9.5: Regulatory and Market Dynamics	137
	9.6: Summary and Conclusion	140
10	Chapter 10: Financial Services and Banking	142
	10.1: Overview of Africa's Financial Sector	142
	10.2: Banking and Microfinance	145
	10.3: Capital Markets and Stock Exchanges	148
	10.4: Insurance and Pension Funds	150
	10.5: Investment in Financial Technology	153
	10.6: Summary and Conclusion	155
11	Chapter 11: The Role of Foreign Direct Investment (FDI)	158
	11.1: Trends in FDI in Africa	158
	11.2: Key Sources of FDI	161
	11.3: Impact of FDI on Economic Development	163
	11.4: Sectoral Distribution of FDI	166
	11.5: Policy Framework for Attracting FDI	168
	11.6: Summary and Conclusion	171
12	Chapter 12: Trade and Regional Integration	174

	12.1: Intra-African Trade and the AfCFTA	174
	12.2: Trade Policies and Agreements	177
	12.3: Regional Trade Blocs	180
	12.4: Trade Infrastructure and Logistics	182
	12.5: Barriers to Trade and Investment	185
	12.7: Summary and Conclusion	188
13	Chapter 13: Social Impact and Responsible Investing	190
	13.1: The Importance of Social Impact Investing	190
	13.2: ESG Criteria in Investment Decisions	193
	3.3: Case Studies of Successful Impact Investments	196
	13.4: Measuring Social and Environmental Impact	198
	13.5: Challenges in Impact Investing	200
	13.6: Summary and Conclusion	202
14	Chapter 14: Case Studies of Successful Investments	204
	14.1: Case Study: Technology Startups	204
	14.3: Case Study: Agribusiness Ventures	206
	14.4: Case Study: Real Estate Development	208
	14.5: Lessons Learned from Failures	210
	14.6: Summary and Conclusion	212
15	Chapter 15: Future Prospects and Strategies for Investors	214
	15.1: Emerging Trends in African Markets	214
	15.2: Strategies for Long-term Investment	216
	15.3: The Role of Innovation in Future Investments	217
	15.4: Leveraging Local Partnerships	219
	15.5: Policy Recommendations for Governments	221
	15.6: Summary and Conclusion	223
About the Author		225

Preface

Welcome to "Africa's Financial Horizon: Opportunities and Challenges for Investors." In this book, we embark on a journey through the dynamic and ever-evolving landscape of African investments, exploring the opportunities, challenges, and strategies that shape the continent's financial future.

Africa is a continent of immense diversity, rich in resources, culture, and potential. From the bustling metropolises of Johannesburg and Cairo to the vibrant markets of Accra and Nairobi, Africa offers a myriad of opportunities for investors seeking growth, innovation, and impact. Yet, navigating the complexities of African markets requires a nuanced understanding of the unique socio-economic, political, and cultural dynamics at play.

In this book, we share our knowledge, wisdom, and practical advice to guide investors on their journey into Africa's financial landscape. From understanding the macroeconomic trends shaping the continent's growth trajectory to identifying key sectors and regions for investment, we provide a comprehensive roadmap for capitalizing on the vast opportunities that Africa offers.

But our journey does not stop there. We also delve into the challenges and risks that investors may encounter, from regulatory hurdles and political instability to currency fluctuations and social dynamics. By equipping readers with a deep understanding of these challenges and offering practical strategies for risk mitigation, we empower investors to make informed decisions and navigate African markets with confidence and resilience.

As we embark on this journey together, we invite you to open your minds and hearts to the possibilities that Africa holds. Whether you are a seasoned investor seeking new frontiers or a newcomer looking to make your mark, "Africa's Financial Horizon" offers a wealth of knowledge, inspiration, and guidance to help you navigate the complexities of African investments and unlock the continent's vast potential.

We hope that this book serves as a valuable companion on your journey into Africa's financial landscape, and that it inspires you to embark on a path of growth, prosperity, and impact in one of the world's most exciting and promising investment destinations.

Warm regards,
Goodson Mumba

Acknowledgments

I would like to eternally and gratefully acknowledge the Almighty God for the infinite intelligence from His universal mind where we draw from all that we come to know and are yet to know. May I also acknowledge and thank everyone that has played a part in my journey of life in terms of spiritual, moral, emotional and material support.

Dedication

I extend my sincerest gratitude to my beloved wife, Edith Mumba, and our children, Angelina, Lubuto, Letticia, Lulumbi, and Butusho, for their unwavering support and understanding throughout the conception, writing, and eventual publication of this book, despite the sacrifices and challenges they endured.

Disclaimer

This book is a work of fiction. Names, characters, businesses, places, events, and incidents are either the products of the author's imagination or used in a fictitious manner. Any resemblance to actual persons, living or dead, or actual events is purely coincidental.

1

Chapter 1: The Decision

1.1: Overview of African Economies

Alex Thompson sat in his high-rise office in New York, staring out at the city skyline. The city that had once felt like the center of the world now seemed small compared to the vast, untapped potential he had glimpsed at the international investment summit. Kwame Mensah's words echoed in his mind: "Africa is not just the future; it is the present."

Determined to explore this new frontier, Alex booked a flight to Johannesburg, South Africa. As the plane descended over the sprawling city, he felt a mixture of excitement and uncertainty. He had read the statistics and reports, but he knew that the real story of Africa's economies would be written in the streets, markets, and boardrooms of its cities.

Upon arrival, Alex was greeted by a bustling metropolis that was both familiar and foreign. Johannesburg's skyline, with its gleaming skyscrapers, contrasted sharply with the vibrant street markets below. He was scheduled to meet with Lindiwe Mkhize, an economist renowned for her insights into African markets.

Lindiwe welcomed him warmly at a chic café in the Sandton district, the economic heart of the city. Over strong African coffee, she began to paint a picture of the continent's diverse economies.

"Africa is not a monolith," she began, her eyes shining with passion. "We have over 50 countries, each with its unique economic landscape. South Africa, where you are now, is one of the continent's largest economies, driven by mining, manufacturing, and services."

As she spoke, Alex could see the energy of the city reflected in her enthusiasm. "But we must also look at Nigeria, the giant of Africa, with its oil wealth and burgeoning tech scene. And Kenya, known as the Silicon Savannah, where innovation is driving financial inclusion and economic growth."

Lindiwe outlined the key sectors across different regions: "West Africa has oil and gas, agriculture is strong in East Africa, and Southern Africa boasts rich mineral resources. Each region offers different opportunities and faces unique challenges."

Alex was struck by the sheer scale and variety of opportunities. He learned about the African Continental Free Trade Area (AfCFTA), which aimed to create a single market for goods and services, fostering intra-African trade and investment. "This could be a game-changer," Lindiwe emphasized. "Imagine the potential when these economies are more integrated."

As they strolled through Sandton, Lindiwe pointed out the contrast between developed areas and those still struggling with poverty. "This dichotomy is one of our biggest challenges," she admitted. "But it also highlights the potential for growth and development."

The day ended with a visit to the Johannesburg Stock Exchange, where Alex saw firsthand the dynamism of the African financial markets. He was introduced to Mbali Ndlovu, a venture capitalist who shared her experiences of investing in African startups.

"The key is to understand the local context," Mbali advised. "Partnerships with local businesses and communities are crucial. It's not just about capital; it's about creating value and impact."

That night, as Alex returned to his hotel, he felt a growing sense of purpose. The overview of African economies had given him a solid foundation, but he knew this was just the beginning. His journey through Africa's financial horizon was about to begin in earnest, and he was ready to discover the opportunities and face the challenges head-on.

In his room, Alex began drafting a plan for his next steps. He listed the countries he wanted to visit, the sectors he was most interested in, and the key contacts he needed to make. This was not just a business trip; it was an expedition into the heart of a continent poised for transformation.

As he drifted off to sleep, Alex dreamed of bustling markets, high-tech hubs, and endless savannas. The promise of Africa was vast, and he was ready to embrace its potential, one step at a time.

1.2 Historical Context of Investment in Africa

The next morning, Alex awoke early, energized by the vibrant city outside his window. He had arranged to meet Lindiwe again, this time at the Apartheid Museum, a place she said would give him deeper insight into the historical context that shaped Africa's current economic landscape.

The museum was a striking structure, a testament to South Africa's tumultuous past and its journey toward reconciliation. As they walked through the exhibits, Lindiwe narrated the history of investment in Africa.

"Africa's investment history is complex and deeply intertwined with its colonial past," she began. "Colonial powers exploited the continent's resources, establishing extractive economies that served their interests rather than those of the local populations."

They stopped in front of a display showing maps of Africa carved up by colonial rulers. "These artificial borders ignored ethnic and cultural boundaries, leading to conflicts that still affect us today," Lindiwe explained. "The legacy of colonialism left many African countries with weak infrastructure and institutions, making post-independence development challenging."

As they moved through the museum, Lindiwe pointed out the impact of the independence movements of the mid-20th century. "The 1960s saw a wave of independence across the continent. Nations like Ghana, under leaders like Kwame Nkrumah, sought to break free from colonial economic structures and build self-sustaining economies."

However, the path to economic independence was fraught with obstacles. Alex learned about the Cold War's influence, where African countries became battlegrounds for superpower rivalries, often destabilizing nascent economies.

They paused at an exhibit on the economic policies of the 1980s and 1990s. "Structural adjustment programs imposed by the International Monetary Fund and World Bank aimed to stabilize economies but often led to austerity measures that hurt the poor," Lindiwe noted. "These programs had mixed results, with some countries experiencing growth while others fell deeper into debt and poverty."

The museum also highlighted the recent era of economic reform and regional cooperation. Lindiwe pointed to a section dedicated to the African Union and regional trade blocs. "In the 21st century, there has been a concerted effort to integrate African economies, improve governance, and attract sustainable investment."

Alex was struck by the resilience and determination of African nations to overcome their historical challenges. "It's clear that understanding this history is crucial for any investor looking to engage with Africa today," he remarked.

As they exited the museum, the sun was setting, casting a golden glow over Johannesburg. Lindiwe suggested they visit a nearby rooftop bar to continue their discussion. Over drinks, the conversation turned to contemporary issues.

"Today, African countries are more assertive in seeking investment that benefits their people," Lindiwe said. "Governments are improving regulatory frameworks, and there is a growing emphasis on sustainable and inclusive growth."

She pointed out that many African nations now actively seek to diversify their economies beyond traditional sectors like mining and agriculture. "There's a vibrant entrepreneurial spirit here, driving growth in technology, renewable energy, and services."

Alex reflected on the profound insights he had gained. The historical context of investment in Africa was not just a backdrop; it was a living force that shaped the present and future. He realized that to be a successful investor in Africa, he needed to respect and understand this rich history.

Lindiwe smiled at Alex's contemplative expression. "You've taken the first step by learning about our past. The next step is to engage with the present and build for the future. Africa is ready for investors who are willing to be true partners in its development."

As he walked back to his hotel, Alex felt a renewed sense of purpose. The historical context had given him a deeper appreciation of the challenges and opportunities ahead. He was more determined than ever to approach his investment journey with respect, understanding, and a commitment to making a positive impact.

In his hotel room, Alex began drafting his thoughts, knowing that his understanding of Africa's financial horizon was becoming clearer. The continent's past, with all its complexities, had set the stage for a future full of potential, and he was eager to be a part of it.

1.3 Current Economic Trends

Alex woke up to the buzz of Johannesburg's morning rush, eager to delve into the current economic trends shaping the continent. He had arranged to meet Mbali Ndlovu, the venture capitalist he had met the day before, who had promised to introduce him to key players in the city's bustling business district.

They met at a trendy co-working space in Sandton, a hive

of activity where young entrepreneurs and seasoned investors mingled. The energy was palpable, a microcosm of Africa's economic dynamism.

"Welcome to the heart of Africa's innovation," Mbali said with a smile as they settled into a glass-walled conference room. "To understand where we're headed, you need to see where we are now."

Mbali began by highlighting the continent's impressive growth rates. "Despite global economic challenges, Africa has been home to some of the fastest-growing economies in the world. Countries like Ethiopia, Rwanda, and Ghana have seen significant GDP growth driven by diverse factors."

She pulled up a presentation on her tablet, showing charts and graphs. "Ethiopia, for instance, has been investing heavily in infrastructure. This has spurred industrial growth and attracted foreign direct investment. Rwanda has transformed itself into a tech and service hub, focusing on creating a business-friendly environment."

Alex noted the impressive statistics but was more intrigued by the stories behind them. "What's driving these trends?" he asked.

Mbali explained the factors fueling growth: "One of the biggest drivers is the demographic dividend. Africa has the youngest population in the world. This means a growing labor force and a rising middle class with increasing purchasing power."

She pointed to another chart. "Urbanization is another key trend. Cities like Lagos, Nairobi, and Accra are expanding rapidly, creating new markets and opportunities for businesses. This urban growth fuels demand for housing, infrastructure, and services."

They were joined by Daniel Okoro, an economist with the African Development Bank, who added his insights. "Don't forget the role of technology," he said. "Mobile technology, in particular, has revolutionized sectors like finance and retail. Mobile money platforms like M-Pesa in Kenya have significantly increased financial inclusion."

Alex was fascinated by the breadth of innovation. "It seems like technology is a game-changer."

"Absolutely," Mbali agreed. "Fintech is just one example. There's also a surge in agritech, healthtech, and e-commerce. African startups are leveraging technology to solve local problems, and they're attracting global investors."

Daniel chimed in, "Another important trend is regional integration. The African Continental Free Trade Area (AfCFTA) aims to create the largest free trade area in the world, boosting intra-African trade and investment. This could be transformative."

As they continued their discussion, Alex realized the immense potential these trends represented. But he also understood the challenges. "What about the obstacles?" he asked.

Mbali nodded. "There are still significant challenges: infrastructure deficits, political instability in some regions, and regulatory hurdles. But there's a growing commitment to addressing these issues. Governments are more aware of the need for stable, transparent environments to attract investment."

Daniel added, "Sustainability is also becoming a focal point. Investors and governments are increasingly prioritizing green energy and sustainable practices. This not only addresses environmental concerns but also opens new avenues for investment."

CHAPTER 1: THE DECISION

To provide a concrete example, Mbali suggested they visit a nearby tech incubator. As they walked through the modern facility, they met young entrepreneurs working on innovative solutions to everyday problems. One startup, for instance, was developing solar-powered refrigerators for rural areas, addressing both energy and food preservation challenges.

"This is the future of Africa," Mbali said, gesturing around the room. "A blend of youthful energy, technological innovation, and a commitment to solving real problems. These are the trends shaping our economies today."

That evening, back at his hotel, Alex reflected on the day's revelations. The current economic trends in Africa were not just numbers and charts; they were living, breathing examples of a continent on the rise. The challenges were real, but so were the opportunities.

Alex felt a profound shift in his perspective. He was not just an investor seeking returns but a participant in a larger narrative of growth and transformation. His journey across Africa's financial horizon had only just begun, but already, he could see the immense potential and the exciting road ahead.

With renewed determination, Alex updated his notes, ready to explore further and dive deeper into the opportunities and challenges that lay before him.

1.4 Key Sectors for Investment

Alex's understanding of Africa's economic landscape was growing deeper with each passing day. Today, he was set to explore the key sectors for investment, and Mbali had arranged a series of meetings with industry leaders across different fields. They met early at a bustling café in Maboneng, a vibrant district known for its art and innovation.

"Today, we'll cover four key sectors: agriculture, energy, technology, and infrastructure," Mbali said, as they sipped their coffee. "Each of these sectors offers unique opportunities and faces distinct challenges."

Their first stop was an urban farm on the outskirts of Johannesburg, where they met with Sipho Dlamini, a pioneer in agribusiness. Rows of hydroponic systems and greenhouses stretched out before them, showcasing a blend of traditional farming and modern technology.

"Agriculture is the backbone of many African economies," Sipho explained, guiding them through the lush rows of vegetables. "With over 60% of the world's arable land, Africa has immense potential. But it's not just about land; it's about innovation. We're using technology to increase yields and sustainability."

He showed them a drone used for monitoring crop health. "Precision farming helps us use resources efficiently and improve productivity. There's a huge market for agritech, from irrigation systems to crop monitoring."

Next, they headed to a renewable energy facility on the outskirts of the city. Here, they met Amina Hassan, an expert in sustainable energy solutions. Solar panels glinted in the midday sun, and wind turbines turned slowly in the distance.

"Energy is crucial for development," Amina said, her enthusiasm palpable. "Africa has vast renewable energy resources – solar, wind, hydro, and geothermal. Investing in renewable energy not only meets local energy needs but also addresses global climate goals."

She walked them through the facility, explaining how they were leveraging solar power for rural electrification. "There are also opportunities in off-grid solutions and mini-grids. Many remote areas lack access to the national grid, and renewable energy can bridge that gap."

As the day progressed, they visited a tech hub in the heart of Johannesburg. The space buzzed with young innovators coding, brainstorming, and pitching ideas. They were introduced to Kwesi Owusu, the founder of a successful fintech startup.

"Technology is transforming Africa," Kwesi said, his eyes gleaming with passion. "Mobile penetration is high, and it's driving change in every sector. Fintech, for example, is revolutionizing financial services, making banking accessible to millions who were previously unbanked."

He demonstrated their mobile payment platform, which facilitated transactions in remote areas. "There's also significant growth in healthtech, edtech, and e-commerce. African tech startups are solving local problems with global relevance."

Their final meeting of the day was with an infrastructure development firm. They met with Olivia Nkosi, who oversaw major infrastructure projects across the continent. Blueprints and models of roads, bridges, and railways filled the conference room.

"Infrastructure is the foundation of economic growth," Olivia stated, her voice confident and clear. "Africa needs substantial investments in transportation, utilities, and urban development. These projects create jobs, improve trade, and enhance quality of life."

She highlighted a new high-speed rail project connecting major cities in East Africa. "Public-private partnerships are key. Governments are increasingly open to collaborating with private investors to meet the infrastructure deficit."

As Alex took in all the information, he felt a sense of awe

at the diverse opportunities across these sectors. Each one held immense potential, driven by innovative solutions and a strong desire for growth and development.

The day ended with a rooftop dinner, overlooking the Johannesburg skyline. Mbali raised her glass. "To Africa's bright future and the endless possibilities that lie ahead. It's investors like you, Alex, who can make a real difference."

Alex clinked his glass with hers, reflecting on the day's insights. The key sectors for investment in Africa were not just areas of economic activity; they were vibrant, dynamic fields ripe with opportunity and innovation. He felt more inspired than ever to contribute to this growth story.

Back in his hotel room, Alex meticulously documented his findings, outlining strategies and potential partnerships. The decision to invest in Africa was not just about financial returns; it was about being part of a transformative journey. The key sectors he had explored today were just the beginning of what promised to be an exciting and rewarding adventure.

1.5 Regional Economic Communities and Trade Blocs

The morning air was crisp as Alex made his way to the headquarters of the African Union's Southern African regional office in Pretoria. Today, he was set to meet with Dr. Nia Simelane, an expert in regional economic communities (RECs) and trade blocs, who would help him understand how these entities were shaping the investment landscape in Africa.

Dr. Simelane greeted Alex warmly and led him into a spacious conference room adorned with maps and flags representing different African countries. "Regional integration is vital for Africa's economic future," she began, gesturing to a map highlighting various RECs. "These communities and trade blocs are designed to foster cooperation and boost economic growth."

She started with the Southern African Development Community (SADC), a bloc comprising 16 countries. "SADC aims to promote sustainable and equitable economic growth and socio-economic development. By facilitating free trade among member states, it reduces barriers and creates larger markets for businesses."

Dr. Simelane pointed to another region on the map. "In East Africa, we have the East African Community (EAC). This is one of the most advanced RECs, with member states working towards greater economic integration, including plans for a common currency. The EAC has significantly improved intra-regional trade and mobility."

Alex listened intently as she moved on to West Africa. "The Economic Community of West African States (ECOWAS) is another major bloc, with 15 member countries. ECOWAS focuses on regional economic integration and development, aiming to create a borderless region where goods, services, and people can move freely."

Dr. Simelane then highlighted the North African region. "The Arab Maghreb Union (AMU) seeks to achieve economic unity among North African countries. Although progress has been slower here due to political challenges, there are ongoing efforts to enhance cooperation."

Alex was struck by the ambition and scope of these organizations. "How do these communities interact with broader continental initiatives?" he asked.

"That's where the African Continental Free Trade Area (AfCFTA) comes in," Dr. Simelane replied, her eyes lighting up with enthusiasm. "AfCFTA is the most significant milestone in Africa's integration agenda. It aims to create a single market for goods and services across the continent, significantly boosting trade and investment."

She showed Alex a chart depicting the potential economic impact of AfCFTA. "By reducing tariffs and non-tariff barriers, AfCFTA is expected to increase intra-African trade by over 50%. This creates a more attractive environment for investors, offering access to a market of over 1.2 billion people."

Dr. Simelane's assistant handed Alex a detailed report on the progress of AfCFTA. "This is a game-changer," she continued. "It's not just about trade; it's about fostering industrialization, creating jobs, and enhancing competitiveness. For investors, it means more predictable and harmonized regulations across borders."

To provide a practical example, Dr. Simelane arranged for Alex to meet with a logistics company that had expanded its operations thanks to SADC's trade facilitation measures. They visited the company's state-of-the-art warehouse in Pretoria, where the CEO, Tshepo Mokoena, explained how regional integration had transformed his business.

"Before SADC's trade agreements, moving goods across borders was a logistical nightmare," Tshepo said, showing Alex the automated systems tracking shipments. "Now, we benefit from streamlined customs procedures and reduced tariffs. This efficiency has allowed us to scale up operations and reach new markets."

The warehouse buzzed with activity as workers prepared shipments bound for neighboring countries. "This level of integration is what makes Africa such an exciting investment destination," Tshepo continued. "The barriers are coming down, and the opportunities are growing exponentially."

Later, as they toured the bustling port of Durban, one of Africa's busiest ports, Dr. Simelane emphasized the importance of infrastructure in supporting regional trade. "Ports, railways, and highways are critical. SADC and other RECs are investing heavily in infrastructure to facilitate trade. This not only boosts regional economies but also attracts foreign investment."

As the day came to a close, Alex felt a deep sense of appreciation for the intricate web of regional communities and trade blocs working to unify the continent's economies. The vision of a connected, prosperous Africa seemed within reach, driven by collaboration and shared goals.

Back at his hotel, Alex summarized his insights. Understanding the role of regional economic communities and trade blocs was essential for any investor looking to tap into Africa's potential. These entities not only enhanced market access but also provided a framework for stability and growth.

Alex felt a renewed confidence in his decision to invest in Africa. The groundwork laid by these communities and trade blocs was creating an environment ripe for opportunity. With each piece of the puzzle coming together, he could see a clearer path forward, ready to navigate the dynamic and promising landscape of Africa's financial horizon.

1.6 Summary and Conclusion

As the sun set over Johannesburg, casting a golden hue across the city, Alex sat on the balcony of his hotel room, reflecting on the whirlwind of insights and experiences from the past few days. His journey through the intricacies of African economies, historical contexts, current trends, key sectors, and regional integration had been nothing short of enlightening.

He took a deep breath and began to summarize his thoughts.

The overview of African economies had revealed a landscape as diverse as it was promising. From South Africa's industrial prowess to Kenya's tech innovations, and Nigeria's oil wealth to Rwanda's rapid transformation, each country offered unique opportunities and faced distinct challenges. The sheer potential of the continent, underpinned by its young population and vast natural resources, was undeniable.

The historical context of investment had provided a critical foundation. Understanding Africa's colonial past, the struggles for independence, and the subsequent economic policies of the 20th century was crucial. It highlighted the resilience and determination of African nations to carve out their own economic destinies, overcoming numerous obstacles along the way.

Current economic trends painted a picture of a continent on the rise. The demographic dividend, rapid urbanization, technological innovation, and regional integration efforts were driving growth and creating new markets. The entrepreneurial spirit and innovative solutions emerging across Africa were testament to its dynamic and evolving economies.

Exploring key sectors for investment had been particularly illuminating. Agriculture, with its blend of traditional practices and modern technology, held immense promise. Renewable energy was poised to revolutionize the energy landscape, while technology startups were solving local problems with global relevance. Infrastructure development remained critical, laying the foundation for sustained economic growth.

The role of regional economic communities and trade blocs

underscored the importance of collaboration and integration. Organizations like SADC, EAC, ECOWAS, and AfCFTA were breaking down barriers, creating larger markets, and fostering economic cooperation. These efforts were transforming Africa into a more attractive and unified investment destination.

As he reviewed his notes, Alex felt a sense of accomplishment. He had come to Africa seeking opportunities, but he had found something far more profound. He had discovered a continent brimming with potential, driven by a spirit of innovation, resilience, and unity.

He picked up his phone and called Lindiwe, Mbali, and Dr. Simelane, inviting them to join him for dinner. As they gathered at a rooftop restaurant, overlooking the twinkling lights of Johannesburg, Alex raised his glass in a toast.

"To Africa's financial horizon," he said, smiling at his new friends. "Thank you for sharing your knowledge, your passion, and your vision. I am honored to be part of this journey."

Lindiwe, Mbali, and Dr. Simelane clinked their glasses with his, their faces reflecting the optimism and excitement that Alex now felt.

Over dinner, they discussed future projects, potential partnerships, and the next steps in Alex's investment journey. The conversation was filled with ideas, laughter, and a shared commitment to making a positive impact on the continent.

That night, as Alex walked back to his hotel, he felt a profound sense of purpose. The decision to invest in Africa was no longer just a business strategy; it was a commitment to being part of a transformative narrative. The challenges were real, but so were the opportunities. With the insights he had gained and the connections he had made, Alex was ready to embrace the journey ahead.

In his room, he sat down to write the conclusion of his first chapter. He wanted to capture the essence of his experiences, the lessons learned, and the vision for the future.

Conclusion:

Alex closed his laptop, feeling a deep sense of fulfillment. He had embarked on this journey to explore Africa's financial horizon, and he had found a world of possibilities. The road ahead would be challenging, but he was ready, armed with knowledge, connections, and a renewed sense of purpose. The future of Africa was bright, and he was honored to play a part in its unfolding story.

Investment Types and Vehicles

Alex sat in the elegant boardroom of a top-tier investment firm in Nairobi, eager to delve into the intricacies of investment types and vehicles in Africa. He was joined by David Mwangi, a seasoned investment advisor with a wealth of experience in the African market.

"Welcome, Alex," David said, extending his hand with a warm smile. "Today, we'll explore the diverse landscape of investment opportunities available across the continent."

Alex nodded, his curiosity piqued. "I'm eager to learn more," he replied.

David began by outlining the various investment types commonly found in Africa. "Investors have a wide range of options, from traditional assets like stocks and bonds to alternative investments such as private equity, venture capital, and real estate."

He elaborated on each type, explaining their characteristics and potential risks and rewards. "Stock markets in Africa are growing, offering opportunities for investors to participate in the region's economic growth. Bonds provide a more stable income stream, while private equity and venture capital offer higher potential returns but come with greater risk."

Alex listened intently, taking notes as David spoke. He was struck by the diversity of investment options and the potential they held for generating returns and making a positive impact.

As they moved on to discuss investment vehicles, David highlighted the importance of choosing the right structure to suit investors' objectives and risk profiles. "Mutual funds and exchange-traded funds (ETFs) offer diversification and professional management, making them attractive options for retail investors."

He pointed out the growing popularity of impact investing, where investors seek to generate both financial returns and positive social or environmental impact. "Impact funds focus on sectors like clean energy, healthcare, and education, aligning with the UN Sustainable Development Goals."

Real estate investment trusts (REITs) were another vehicle David emphasized, particularly in markets like South Africa and Nigeria. "REITs provide exposure to the property market without the hassle of direct ownership. They offer attractive dividends and capital appreciation potential."

As the discussion unfolded, Alex felt a sense of excitement building within him. The breadth of investment options and vehicles presented a vast landscape of possibilities, each offering its own unique set of opportunities and challenges.

To provide a practical illustration, David arranged for Alex to meet with a portfolio manager overseeing a diversified investment fund. They visited the firm's offices in the bustling business district of Nairobi, where Alex had the opportunity to learn firsthand about their investment strategy and approach.

The portfolio manager walked him through their investment process, emphasizing rigorous due diligence and risk management. "We focus on identifying high-growth sectors and companies with strong fundamentals," he explained. "Our goal is to generate attractive returns for our investors while contributing to the sustainable development of the region."

Alex was impressed by the depth of expertise and professionalism displayed by the investment team. He saw how their disciplined approach to investing could mitigate risks and capitalize on opportunities in the dynamic African market.

As the day drew to a close, Alex thanked David for his insights and guidance. He left the investment firm with a newfound appreciation for the diverse range of investment types and vehicles available in Africa.

Back at his hotel, Alex reflected on the day's discussions. Understanding the investment landscape was essential for navigating the complexities of the African market. Armed with this knowledge, he felt better equipped to make informed decisions and seize opportunities that aligned with his investment goals.

With a sense of purpose and determination, Alex prepared to delve deeper into the investment landscape, knowing that each investment type and vehicle held the potential to shape his journey through Africa's financial horizon.

2

Chapter 2: Understanding the Investment Landscape

2.1: Investment Types and Vehicles

Alex sat in the elegant boardroom of a top-tier investment firm in Nairobi, eager to delve into the intricacies of investment types and vehicles in Africa. He was joined by David Mwangi, a seasoned investment advisor with a wealth of experience in the African market.

"Welcome, Alex," David said, extending his hand with a warm smile. "Today, we'll explore the diverse landscape of investment opportunities available across the continent."

Alex nodded, his curiosity piqued. "I'm eager to learn more," he replied.

David began by outlining the various investment types commonly found in Africa. "Investors have a wide range of options, from traditional assets like stocks and bonds to alternative investments such as private equity, venture capital, and real estate."

He elaborated on each type, explaining their characteristics and potential risks and rewards. "Stock markets in Africa are growing, offering opportunities for investors to participate in the region's economic growth. Bonds provide a more stable income stream, while private equity and venture capital offer higher potential returns but come with greater risk."

Alex listened intently, taking notes as David spoke. He was struck by the diversity of investment options and the potential they held for generating returns and making a positive impact.

As they moved on to discuss investment vehicles, David highlighted the importance of choosing the right structure to suit investors' objectives and risk profiles. "Mutual funds and exchange-traded funds (ETFs) offer diversification and professional management, making them attractive options for retail investors."

He pointed out the growing popularity of impact investing, where investors seek to generate both financial returns and positive social or environmental impact. "Impact funds focus on sectors like clean energy, healthcare, and education, aligning with the UN Sustainable Development Goals."

Real estate investment trusts (REITs) were another vehicle David emphasized, particularly in markets like South Africa and Nigeria. "REITs provide exposure to the property market without the hassle of direct ownership. They offer attractive dividends and capital appreciation potential."

As the discussion unfolded, Alex felt a sense of excitement building within him. The breadth of investment options and vehicles presented a vast landscape of possibilities, each offering its own unique set of opportunities and challenges.

To provide a practical illustration, David arranged for Alex to meet with a portfolio manager overseeing a diversified investment fund. They visited the firm's offices in the bustling business district of Nairobi, where Alex had the opportunity to learn firsthand about their investment strategy and approach.

The portfolio manager walked him through their investment process, emphasizing rigorous due diligence and risk management. "We focus on identifying high-growth sectors and companies with strong fundamentals," he explained. "Our goal is to generate attractive returns for our investors while contributing to the sustainable development of the region."

Alex was impressed by the depth of expertise and professionalism displayed by the investment team. He saw how their disciplined approach to investing could mitigate risks and capitalize on opportunities in the dynamic African market.

As the day drew to a close, Alex thanked David for his insights and guidance. He left the investment firm with a newfound appreciation for the diverse range of investment types and vehicles available in Africa.

Back at his hotel, Alex reflected on the day's discussions. Understanding the investment landscape was essential for navigating the complexities of the African market. Armed with this knowledge, he felt better equipped to make informed decisions and seize opportunities that aligned with his investment goals.

With a sense of purpose and determination, Alex prepared to delve deeper into the investment landscape, knowing that each investment type and vehicle held the potential to shape his journey through Africa's financial horizon.

2.2 Regulatory Environment

The next morning, Alex found himself in the bustling capital city of Accra, Ghana, ready to explore the regulatory environment shaping investment across Africa. He was scheduled to meet with Ama Serwah, a legal expert specializing in investment law and regulation.

Ama greeted Alex warmly as they sat down in her office overlooking the city skyline. "Navigating the regulatory landscape is crucial for investors looking to operate in Africa," she began, her voice confident and assured. "Each country has its own set of laws and regulations governing investment, and understanding these nuances is essential for success."

She explained that while Africa offered vast opportunities, the regulatory environment could be complex and challenging to navigate. "Investors must be aware of local laws, regulations, and licensing requirements," Ama emphasized. "Compliance is key to avoiding legal pitfalls and ensuring a smooth investment process."

Ama outlined the key regulatory considerations for investors, ranging from company registration and taxation to foreign exchange controls and intellectual property rights protection. "Investors should conduct thorough due diligence and seek legal advice to ensure compliance with local regulations," she advised.

To provide a practical example, Ama arranged for Alex to meet with a team of lawyers specializing in investment law. They discussed recent regulatory changes in Ghana, including reforms aimed at streamlining business registration processes and improving transparency and investor protection.

Alex listened intently as the lawyers explained the intricacies of Ghana's investment landscape, highlighting the importance of building strong relationships with local authorities and stakeholders. "Understanding the regulatory environment is essential for building trust and credibility," they emphasized.

As they toured the city, Ama pointed out various government agencies responsible for overseeing investment activities. "Investors should familiarize themselves with these institutions and establish open lines of communication," she explained. "Engaging with regulators proactively can help address any concerns or issues that may arise."

Later that afternoon, Ama arranged for Alex to attend a seminar on investment law and regulation hosted by the Ghana Investment Promotion Centre (GIPC). The event brought together investors, government officials, and legal experts to discuss regulatory reforms and best practices for attracting investment.

Alex found the seminar insightful, gaining valuable insights into Ghana's investment climate and the government's efforts to create a more conducive environment for investors. He was impressed by the commitment to transparency, accountability, and investor protection demonstrated by both the public and private sectors.

As the day came to a close, Alex thanked Ama for her guidance and expertise. He left her office feeling more confident in his ability to navigate the regulatory challenges of investing in Africa.

Back at his hotel, Alex reflected on the day's discussions. The regulatory environment was a critical factor in shaping investment decisions, and understanding its complexities was essential for success. Armed with this knowledge, he felt better prepared to navigate the legal landscape and seize opportunities that aligned with his investment goals.

With a renewed sense of purpose, Alex prepared to continue his journey through Africa's investment landscape, knowing that a solid understanding of the regulatory environment would be crucial every step of the way.

2.3 Legal Frameworks for Investors

The sun was just beginning to rise over the skyline of Lagos, Nigeria, as Alex made his way to meet with Tunde Olatunji, a leading expert in legal frameworks for investors in Africa. As he entered Tunde's office, he was greeted by the warm smile of a man who exuded confidence and authority.

"Welcome, Alex," Tunde said, motioning for him to take a seat. "Today, we'll explore the legal frameworks that govern investment activities across Africa."

Alex listened intently as Tunde began to outline the legal structures and protections available to investors. "Africa offers a variety of legal frameworks designed to attract and protect investment," he explained. "These include investment laws, bilateral investment treaties (BITs), and international arbitration mechanisms."

He emphasized the importance of understanding the legal framework in each country where investors operate. "Investment laws vary from one country to another, so it's essential to conduct thorough due diligence and seek legal advice to ensure compliance and mitigate risks," Tunde advised.

As they delved deeper into the discussion, Tunde highlighted the role of BITs in providing additional protections for investors. "BITs are agreements between two countries that establish reciprocal rights and obligations related to investment," he explained. "They typically include provisions on expropriation, compensation, and dispute resolution."

To provide a practical example, Tunde arranged for Alex to meet with a team of lawyers specializing in international arbitration. They discussed the importance of dispute resolution mechanisms in protecting investors' rights and interests.

"International arbitration provides a neutral and impartial forum for resolving investment disputes," the lawyers explained. "It offers investors greater certainty and predictability, reducing the risks associated with investing in emerging markets."

As they toured the city, Tunde pointed out various landmarks symbolizing Nigeria's commitment to legal frameworks for investors. "Nigeria has made significant strides in strengthening its legal and regulatory environment to attract investment," he noted. "The government has implemented reforms aimed at enhancing transparency, efficiency, and investor protection."

Later that afternoon, Tunde arranged for Alex to attend a conference on investment law and international arbitration. The event brought together legal experts, government officials, and investors to discuss best practices and emerging trends in investment arbitration.

Alex found the conference enlightening, gaining valuable insights into the legal frameworks and protections available to investors in Africa. He was impressed by the level of expertise and professionalism demonstrated by the speakers and participants.

As the day came to a close, Alex thanked Tunde for his guidance and expertise. He left Tunde's office feeling more confident in his understanding of the legal landscape and its implications for investment activities in Africa.

Back at his hotel, Alex reflected on the day's discussions. The legal frameworks for investors were a crucial aspect of the investment landscape, providing protections and safeguards against potential risks. Armed with this knowledge, he felt better prepared to navigate the legal complexities and seize opportunities that aligned with his investment goals.

With a renewed sense of purpose, Alex prepared to continue his journey through Africa's investment landscape, knowing that a solid understanding of legal frameworks would be essential every step of the way.

2.4 Financial Institutions and Market Infrastructure

As the sun reached its zenith over the skyline of Johannesburg, Alex found himself in the heart of the city's financial district, ready to explore the role of financial institutions and market infrastructure in shaping investment across Africa. He was scheduled to meet with Thabo Moloi, a seasoned banker with decades of experience in the African financial sector.

Thabo greeted Alex with a firm handshake and led him into a sleek conference room overlooking the bustling streets below. "Welcome, Alex," he said, gesturing for him to take a seat. "Today, we'll delve into the role of financial institutions and market infrastructure in facilitating investment activities."

Alex listened intently as Thabo began to explain the importance of financial institutions in providing essential services to investors. "Financial institutions play a critical role in mobilizing capital, facilitating transactions, and managing risk," Thabo explained. "From commercial banks and investment firms to stock exchanges and regulatory bodies, these institutions form

CHAPTER 2: UNDERSTANDING THE INVESTMENT LANDSCAPE

the backbone of the financial ecosystem."

He elaborated on the various types of financial institutions found across Africa, highlighting their functions and responsibilities. "Commercial banks provide a wide range of banking services, including lending, deposit-taking, and foreign exchange transactions," Thabo said. "Investment firms, on the other hand, specialize in asset management, securities trading, and advisory services."

As they delved deeper into the discussion, Thabo emphasized the importance of market infrastructure in supporting investment activities. "Market infrastructure refers to the systems and institutions that facilitate the trading of financial assets," he explained. "This includes stock exchanges, clearing and settlement systems, and regulatory frameworks."

To provide a practical example, Thabo arranged for Alex to visit the Johannesburg Stock Exchange (JSE), one of Africa's largest and most established stock exchanges. They toured the exchange's trading floor, where Alex had the opportunity to observe firsthand the excitement and energy of the trading floor.

"The JSE plays a vital role in providing liquidity and price discovery for investors," Thabo explained as they watched traders execute buy and sell orders. "It serves as a platform for companies to raise capital and for investors to buy and sell shares in listed companies."

Later that afternoon, Thabo arranged for Alex to meet with executives from a leading investment firm specializing in African markets. They discussed the role of financial institutions in supporting investment activities and the importance of market infrastructure in facilitating efficient and transparent markets.

"As an investor, it's essential to have access to reliable financial institutions and robust market infrastructure," one executive explained. "These institutions provide the necessary tools and services to navigate the complexities of the African market and capitalize on investment opportunities."

As the day came to a close, Alex thanked Thabo for his insights and guidance. He left the financial district feeling more enlightened about the role of financial institutions and market infrastructure in shaping investment activities across Africa.

Back at his hotel, Alex reflected on the day's discussions. The financial institutions and market infrastructure were critical components of the investment landscape, providing the necessary support and infrastructure for investors to thrive. Armed with this knowledge, he felt better prepared to navigate the complexities of the African market and seize opportunities that aligned with his investment goals.

With a renewed sense of confidence, Alex prepared to continue his journey through Africa's investment landscape, knowing that financial institutions and market infrastructure would play a crucial role in shaping his investment decisions every step of the way.

2.5 Key Investment Policies and Reforms

As the sun began to set over the skyline of Nairobi, Alex found himself in the midst of a lively discussion with Grace Mwangi, an expert in investment policies and reforms in Africa. They sat in a cozy café, surrounded by the vibrant energy of the city.

"Welcome, Alex," Grace said, her voice filled with warmth. "Today, we'll explore the key investment policies and reforms shaping the investment landscape across Africa."

Alex nodded eagerly, ready to delve into this crucial aspect of investment. Grace began by outlining the importance of investment policies in creating an attractive environment for investors. "Investment policies play a crucial role in attracting capital, fostering economic growth, and promoting sustainable development," she explained. "They provide the framework within which investment activities can thrive."

She elaborated on the various types of investment policies and reforms implemented by African governments, ranging from tax incentives and investment promotion agencies to sector-specific regulations and public-private partnerships. "Governments across Africa are implementing a range of policies and reforms aimed at improving the investment climate and attracting foreign direct investment," Grace said.

As they delved deeper into the discussion, Grace highlighted some of the key investment policies and reforms being implemented in countries across Africa. "Many governments are focusing on streamlining business registration processes, reducing bureaucratic red tape, and improving the ease of doing business," she explained. "These reforms aim to create a more conducive environment for investment, reduce barriers to entry, and promote entrepreneurship and innovation."

To provide a practical example, Grace arranged for Alex to meet with a government official responsible for investment promotion in Kenya. They discussed the various policies and reforms being implemented by the Kenyan government to attract investment and stimulate economic growth.

"The Kenyan government has implemented a range of measures to promote investment, including tax incentives, infrastructure development, and regulatory reforms," the official explained. "We are committed to creating an enabling environment for investors and ensuring that Kenya remains a competitive destination for investment."

Later that evening, Grace arranged for Alex to attend a conference on investment policies and reforms in Africa. The event brought together government officials, policymakers, and investors to discuss best practices and emerging trends in investment promotion and regulation.

Alex found the conference enlightening, gaining valuable insights into the various policies and reforms being implemented across Africa to attract investment. He was impressed by the commitment of African governments to creating a conducive environment for investment and promoting economic growth and development.

As the night drew to a close, Alex thanked Grace for her insights and guidance. He left the café feeling more enlightened about the importance of investment policies and reforms in shaping the investment landscape across Africa.

Back at his hotel, Alex reflected on the day's discussions. The key investment policies and reforms being implemented across Africa were essential for creating an attractive environment for investors and stimulating economic growth and development. Armed with this knowledge, he felt better prepared to navigate the complexities of the African market and seize opportunities that aligned with his investment goals.

With a renewed sense of optimism, Alex prepared to continue his journey through Africa's investment landscape, knowing that key investment policies and reforms would play a crucial role in shaping his investment decisions every step of the way.

2.6 Summary and Conclusion

As the city lights sparkled against the night sky of Cape Town, Alex sat down to reflect on the wealth of knowledge he had gained throughout the day. He was ready to synthesize the insights from his discussions on key investment policies and reforms into a comprehensive understanding of Africa's investment landscape.

Taking out his notebook, Alex began to summarize the key points:

"The investment landscape in Africa is shaped by a variety of factors, including investment types and vehicles, regulatory environment, legal frameworks, financial institutions and market infrastructure, and key investment policies and reforms."

He paused, allowing the words to sink in. Each aspect played a crucial role in shaping the opportunities and challenges faced by investors in Africa.

"Understanding the different investment types and vehicles available allows investors to tailor their strategies to their specific objectives and risk profiles. Meanwhile, navigating the regulatory environment and legal frameworks is essential for ensuring compliance and mitigating risks."

Alex continued to jot down his thoughts, highlighting the role of financial institutions and market infrastructure in providing the necessary support and infrastructure for investors to thrive. "Financial institutions such as banks, investment firms, and stock exchanges play a vital role in mobilizing capital, facilitating transactions, and managing risk. Market infrastructure, including stock exchanges and regulatory frameworks, provides the necessary tools and services to navigate the complexities of the African market."

He reflected on the key investment policies and reforms being implemented across Africa, recognizing their importance in creating an attractive environment for investors and stimulating economic growth and development. "Investment policies and reforms, such as tax incentives, infrastructure development, and regulatory reforms, aim to reduce barriers to entry, promote entrepreneurship and innovation, and create a conducive environment for investment."

As Alex closed his notebook, he felt a sense of satisfaction wash over him. The insights he had gained throughout the day had provided him with a deeper understanding of Africa's investment landscape. Armed with this knowledge, he felt better equipped to navigate the complexities of the African market and seize opportunities that aligned with his investment goals.

With a renewed sense of purpose, Alex prepared to continue his journey through Africa's investment landscape, knowing that a comprehensive understanding of the various factors shaping the market would be essential for success.

As he turned off the lights and settled into bed, Alex felt a sense of excitement for the adventures that lay ahead. The road to success in Africa's investment landscape would be challenging, but with the knowledge and insights he had gained, he was ready to embrace the journey with confidence and determination.

3

Chapter 3: Risk Management in African Investments

3.1 Identifying Investment Risks

The sun rose over the sprawling savannah of Tanzania as Alex embarked on the next leg of his journey, delving into the intricacies of risk management in African investments. He was scheduled to meet with Dr. Fatima Kibwana, a renowned risk management expert with extensive experience in the African market.

Dr. Kibwana welcomed Alex into her office, the shelves lined with books on risk analysis and investment strategies. "Good morning, Alex," she greeted him with a warm smile. "Today, we'll explore the importance of identifying investment risks in Africa."

Alex settled into his chair, eager to learn. Dr. Kibwana began by emphasizing the dynamic and diverse nature of investment risks in Africa. "Investing in Africa offers tremendous opportunities, but it also comes with its fair share of risks," she explained. "From political instability and regulatory uncertainty to currency fluctuations and market volatility, investors must be vigilant in identifying and assessing these risks."

She elaborated on the various types of investment risks prevalent in Africa, ranging from macroeconomic risks such as inflation and currency devaluation to microeconomic risks such as industry competition and company-specific factors. "Each investment carries its own unique set of risks, and it's essential for investors to conduct thorough due diligence to identify and understand these risks," Dr. Kibwana emphasized.

To provide a practical example, Dr. Kibwana arranged for Alex to meet with a team of risk analysts at a leading investment firm. They discussed the methodologies and tools used to identify and assess investment risks, including scenario analysis, stress testing, and risk modeling.

"As risk analysts, our job is to identify potential threats to investment performance and develop strategies to mitigate these risks," one analyst explained. "We analyze a wide range of factors, including political, economic, and social developments, to anticipate and respond to emerging risks."

As they delved deeper into the discussion, Dr. Kibwana highlighted the importance of conducting country-specific risk assessments when investing in Africa. "Each country presents its own unique set of risks and opportunities," she said. "Investors must consider factors such as political stability, regulatory environment, and economic growth prospects when evaluating investment opportunities."

Later that afternoon, Dr. Kibwana arranged for Alex to attend a seminar on risk management in African investments. The event brought together risk management professionals, investors, and policymakers to discuss best practices and emerging trends in risk analysis and mitigation.

Alex found the seminar enlightening, gaining valuable insights into the complexities of risk management in African investments. He was impressed by the level of expertise and sophistication demonstrated by the speakers and participants.

As the day came to a close, Alex thanked Dr. Kibwana for her insights and guidance. He left her office feeling more enlightened about the importance of identifying investment risks in Africa and the methodologies used to assess and mitigate these risks.

Back at his hotel, Alex reflected on the day's discussions. Identifying investment risks was a crucial step in managing investment portfolios effectively. Armed with this knowledge, he felt better equipped to navigate the complexities of the African market and make informed investment decisions that aligned with his risk tolerance and objectives.

With a renewed sense of purpose, Alex prepared to continue his journey through Africa's investment landscape, knowing that a thorough understanding of investment risks would be essential for success in the dynamic and challenging environment of African investments.

3.2: Political and Economic Risks

As the morning sun bathed the skyline of Nairobi in golden light, Alex prepared to delve deeper into the complexities of risk management in African investments. He was scheduled to meet with Dr. Joseph Kamau, a seasoned political economist with a wealth of experience in analyzing political and economic risks in the region.

Dr. Kamau welcomed Alex into his office, adorned with maps and charts depicting the political and economic landscape of Africa. "Good morning, Alex," he greeted him with a firm handshake. "Today, we'll explore the political and economic risks that investors face when investing in Africa."

Alex nodded attentively, eager to learn from Dr. Kamau's expertise. Dr. Kamau began by emphasizing the interconnectedness of political and economic factors in shaping investment risks. "Political stability and economic performance are closely intertwined," he explained. "Political instability can lead to economic uncertainty, while economic downturns can exacerbate political tensions."

He elaborated on the various political risks prevalent in Africa, ranging from civil unrest and government instability to regulatory changes and corruption. "Investors must carefully assess the political environment in each country where they operate," Dr. Kamau advised. "Factors such as government policies, rule of law, and civil liberties can significantly impact investment outcomes."

To provide a practical example, Dr. Kamau arranged for Alex to meet with a group of political analysts specializing in African politics. They discussed recent political developments in the region, including elections, protests, and government reforms, and their implications for investors.

"As political analysts, our job is to monitor political developments and assess their potential impact on investment risks," one analyst explained. "We analyze factors such as government stability, policy continuity, and social cohesion to provide insights into the political environment."

As they delved deeper into the discussion, Dr. Kamau highlighted the importance of understanding economic risks

CHAPTER 3: RISK MANAGEMENT IN AFRICAN INVESTMENTS

in African investments. "Economic factors such as inflation, exchange rate volatility, and fiscal deficits can pose significant challenges for investors," he said. "Economic downturns can lead to reduced consumer spending, declining asset values, and increased business failures."

Later that afternoon, Dr. Kamau arranged for Alex to attend a seminar on political and economic risks in African investments. The event brought together economists, political analysts, and investors to discuss best practices and emerging trends in risk analysis and mitigation.

Alex found the seminar enlightening, gaining valuable insights into the complexities of political and economic risks in African investments. He was impressed by the level of expertise and depth of analysis demonstrated by the speakers and participants.

As the day came to a close, Alex thanked Dr. Kamau for his insights and guidance. He left his office feeling more enlightened about the political and economic risks that investors face when investing in Africa.

Back at his hotel, Alex reflected on the day's discussions. Political and economic risks were inherent in African investments, but with careful analysis and risk management strategies, investors could navigate these challenges effectively. Armed with this knowledge, he felt better prepared to assess investment opportunities and make informed decisions that aligned with his risk tolerance and objectives.

With a renewed sense of determination, Alex prepared to continue his journey through Africa's investment landscape, knowing that a thorough understanding of political and economic risks would be essential for success in the dynamic and evolving market of African investments.

3.3: Currency and Exchange Rate Risks

As the day unfolded in the bustling city of Johannesburg, Alex's quest to unravel the intricacies of risk management in African investments led him to explore the nuances of currency and exchange rate risks. He was scheduled to meet with Dr. Nomvula Ndlovu, a renowned economist specializing in currency markets and exchange rate dynamics.

Dr. Ndlovu welcomed Alex into her office, adorned with charts and graphs illustrating currency fluctuations and exchange rate trends. "Good afternoon, Alex," she greeted him warmly. "Today, we'll delve into the critical role that currency and exchange rate risks play in shaping investment outcomes in Africa."

Alex settled into his chair, eager to gain insights from Dr. Ndlovu's expertise. She began by explaining the significance of currency risks in African investments. "Currency fluctuations can have a profound impact on investment returns, especially for investors operating across borders," Dr. Ndlovu explained. "Changes in exchange rates can affect the value of investment assets and the cost of doing business."

She elaborated on the various factors influencing currency and exchange rate risks, including monetary policy decisions, macroeconomic fundamentals, and global market dynamics. "Investors must carefully monitor currency markets and assess the potential impact of exchange rate movements on their investment portfolios," Dr. Ndlovu advised.

To provide a practical example, Dr. Ndlovu arranged for Alex to meet with a team of currency analysts at a leading financial institution. They discussed recent trends in currency markets, including the impact of geopolitical events and economic data releases on exchange rates.

"As currency analysts, our job is to analyze the factors driving exchange rate movements and provide insights into potential risks and opportunities for investors," one analyst explained. "We use a combination of technical analysis, fundamental analysis, and market sentiment to forecast currency trends and inform investment decisions."

As they delved deeper into the discussion, Dr. Ndlovu highlighted the importance of implementing risk management strategies to mitigate currency and exchange rate risks. "Investors can use various hedging techniques, such as forward contracts, options, and currency swaps, to protect their portfolios from adverse exchange rate movements," she said.

Later that afternoon, Dr. Ndlovu arranged for Alex to attend a seminar on currency and exchange rate risks in African investments. The event brought together economists, currency analysts, and investors to discuss best practices and emerging trends in currency risk management.

Alex found the seminar enlightening, gaining valuable insights into the complexities of currency and exchange rate risks in African investments. He was impressed by the level of expertise and depth of analysis demonstrated by the speakers and participants.

As the day came to a close, Alex thanked Dr. Ndlovu for her insights and guidance. He left her office feeling more enlightened about the currency and exchange rate risks that investors face when investing in Africa.

Back at his hotel, Alex reflected on the day's discussions. Currency and exchange rate risks were significant considerations for investors operating in Africa, but with careful analysis and risk management strategies, these challenges could be mitigated effectively. Armed with this knowledge, he felt better prepared to navigate the complexities of the African market and make informed investment decisions that aligned with his risk tolerance and objectives.

With a renewed sense of confidence, Alex prepared to continue his journey through Africa's investment landscape, knowing that a thorough understanding of currency and exchange rate risks would be essential for success in the dynamic and evolving market of African investments.

3.4: Social and Cultural Risks

As the sun dipped below the horizon, casting a warm glow over the vibrant city of Lagos, Alex delved deeper into the complexities of risk management in African investments. His next stop was a meeting with Dr. Ngozi Adeniyi, a cultural anthropologist specializing in social and cultural risks in the African context.

Dr. Adeniyi welcomed Alex into her office, adorned with artifacts and paintings reflecting the rich cultural tapestry of Africa. "Good evening, Alex," she greeted him with a bright smile. "Today, we'll explore the often-overlooked yet critical aspect of social and cultural risks in African investments."

Alex settled into his chair, intrigued by the prospect of understanding how social and cultural factors could impact investment outcomes. Dr. Adeniyi began by emphasizing the importance of considering the social and cultural context when assessing investment risks. "Social and cultural dynamics can have a profound impact on business operations and investor relations," she explained. "Factors such as language barriers, cultural norms, and social hierarchies can affect the success or failure of investment ventures."

She elaborated on the various types of social and cultural risks prevalent in Africa, ranging from community resistance to foreign investment to labor disputes and employee relations issues. "Investors must be sensitive to the social and cultural context in which they operate and take proactive measures to mitigate potential risks," Dr. Adeniyi advised.

To provide a practical example, Dr. Adeniyi arranged for Alex to meet with a group of local community leaders in a rural village outside Lagos. They discussed the challenges and opportunities associated with foreign investment in their community, addressing concerns related to land rights, environmental conservation, and economic development.

"As community leaders, our primary concern is the well-being and prosperity of our people," one leader explained. "We welcome investment that benefits our community, but it must be done in a way that respects our cultural values and traditions."

As they delved deeper into the discussion, Dr. Adeniyi highlighted the importance of building strong relationships with local communities and stakeholders to mitigate social and cultural risks. "Investors must engage in meaningful dialogue with local communities and seek to understand their needs and aspirations," she said. "By building trust and fostering mutual respect, investors can mitigate potential conflicts and build sustainable partnerships."

Later that evening, Dr. Adeniyi arranged for Alex to attend a cultural event celebrating the diverse heritage of Nigeria. The event brought together people from different ethnic backgrounds, showcasing traditional music, dance, and cuisine.

Alex found the event enlightening, gaining valuable insights into the rich cultural diversity of Africa and the importance of understanding and respecting local customs and traditions. He was impressed by the warmth and hospitality of the people he met, realizing the significance of social and cultural factors in shaping investment outcomes.

As the night drew to a close, Alex thanked Dr. Adeniyi for her insights and guidance. He left her office feeling more enlightened about the social and cultural risks that investors face when investing in Africa.

Back at his hotel, Alex reflected on the day's discussions. Social and cultural risks were significant considerations for investors operating in Africa, but with careful planning and engagement, these challenges could be addressed effectively. Armed with this knowledge, he felt better prepared to navigate the complexities of the African market and make informed investment decisions that respected local customs and traditions.

With a renewed sense of appreciation for Africa's rich cultural heritage, Alex prepared to continue his journey through the investment landscape, knowing that understanding social and cultural dynamics would be essential for success in the dynamic and diverse markets of Africa.

3.5: Strategies for Risk Mitigation

The conference room was abuzz with activity as investors, analysts, and local partners gathered for the final session of the day. Alex and Ms. Ibrahim had spent the past few hours navigating the complex terrain of investment risks in Africa. Now, it was time to explore the strategies that could mitigate

CHAPTER 3: RISK MANAGEMENT IN AFRICAN INVESTMENTS

these risks and pave the way for sustainable success.

"To mitigate risks effectively, we need a multifaceted approach," began Ms. Ibrahim, addressing the audience with a confident yet measured tone. "It's not just about identifying risks, but also about implementing strategies that turn potential pitfalls into opportunities for growth."

Alex took a deep breath and stepped forward to present their findings. "Our first strategy focuses on diversification," he said, pointing to a slide that displayed a colorful pie chart. "By spreading investments across different sectors, regions, and asset classes, we can reduce exposure to any single risk factor. For example, combining investments in technology, agriculture, and real estate across East, West, and Southern Africa can create a balanced portfolio that is more resilient to local disruptions."

Ms. Ibrahim nodded and added, "Next, we must consider the importance of local partnerships. Collaborating with local businesses, governments, and communities can provide invaluable insights and resources that help navigate the regulatory and cultural landscape. These partnerships also build trust and foster goodwill, which are essential for long-term success."

The audience leaned in, clearly intrigued by the practical insights being shared. Alex continued, "Political risk insurance is another crucial tool. This can protect investments against losses arising from political instability, expropriation, and other government actions that could negatively impact our operations."

Ms. Ibrahim chimed in, "And don't forget about hedging strategies to manage currency and exchange rate risks. Utilizing financial instruments like futures, options, and swaps can help stabilize returns and protect against unfavorable currency fluctuations."

A participant raised a hand. "What about social and cultural risks?" they asked. "How do we address those?"

Ms. Ibrahim smiled. "Great question. Engaging with local communities and understanding their needs and values is key. Corporate social responsibility (CSR) initiatives that focus on social development, education, and healthcare can build strong community relations and enhance our reputation as responsible investors. This not only mitigates social risks but also creates a positive impact."

Alex concluded, "Lastly, ongoing risk assessment and monitoring are vital. Regularly reviewing and adjusting our strategies based on new data and changing conditions ensures that we stay ahead of potential risks and seize emerging opportunities."

The room filled with a sense of cautious optimism as the session wrapped up. Alex and Ms. Ibrahim's presentation had provided a clear roadmap for navigating the complex risk landscape of African investments. As they mingled with attendees afterwards, the conversations were animated and hopeful, filled with new ideas and strategies for mitigating risks and driving growth.

Walking out of the conference center, Alex turned to Ms. Ibrahim. "I think we made a real impact today," he said.

Ms. Ibrahim nodded, a satisfied smile on her face. "Absolutely. By focusing on proactive risk mitigation strategies, we've shown that with careful planning and collaboration, the potential for success in African markets is immense."

With renewed determination, they both knew that their journey was far from over. Together, they were committed to transforming challenges into opportunities and ensuring a prosperous future for investors and communities across Africa.

3.6: Summary and Conclusion

The final rays of sunlight filtered through the large windows of the conference room, casting a warm glow on the faces of the attendees. Alex and Ms. Ibrahim stood side by side at the front of the room, ready to wrap up their intensive discussion on risk management in African investments.

"Before we conclude today's session, let's take a moment to summarize the key points we've covered," Alex began, his voice steady and confident. "We've explored the multifaceted nature of investment risks in Africa, from political and economic uncertainties to currency fluctuations and social dynamics."

Ms. Ibrahim continued, "We've discussed strategies to identify these risks, emphasizing the importance of thorough due diligence and continuous monitoring. We highlighted the value of local partnerships, which provide essential insights and foster trust, and we examined financial tools like political risk insurance and currency hedging to protect against specific threats."

Alex glanced around the room, making eye contact with several participants who were taking notes. "We also delved into the importance of diversification, both geographically and across sectors, to spread risk and enhance portfolio resilience. Furthermore, we stressed the necessity of engaging with local communities through CSR initiatives to mitigate social risks and build a positive reputation."

Ms. Ibrahim added, "Throughout our discussion, we emphasized that risk management is not a one-time effort but an ongoing process. It requires vigilance, adaptability, and a willingness to learn and adjust strategies as conditions evolve."

As they spoke, the energy in the room was palpable. The attendees were clearly engaged, nodding in agreement and jotting down final thoughts. Alex and Ms. Ibrahim's collaborative dynamic had made the complex topic of risk management accessible and actionable.

Alex took a deep breath and delivered the concluding remarks. "In summary, successful investment in Africa hinges on a proactive and comprehensive approach to risk management. By diversifying investments, leveraging local partnerships, utilizing financial protections, and committing to continuous assessment and adaptation, we can turn potential challenges into opportunities for growth and innovation."

Ms. Ibrahim smiled warmly. "Remember, Africa's markets are full of potential, but like any investment landscape, they require careful navigation. With the right strategies, we can mitigate risks and unlock the vast opportunities that this continent offers."

As the session concluded, the room erupted into applause. Attendees approached Alex and Ms. Ibrahim, eager to discuss their insights further and express their appreciation. The atmosphere was charged with optimism and a newfound sense of confidence.

Walking out of the conference center, Alex felt a sense of accomplishment. "I think we've equipped them with the tools they need to succeed," he said.

Ms. Ibrahim nodded in agreement. "Absolutely. By understanding and managing risks, they're better positioned to make impactful and profitable investments in Africa."

The evening air was cool and refreshing as they stepped

outside, their minds already buzzing with plans for the next steps in their journey. Together, they were ready to face the challenges and seize the opportunities that lay ahead in the dynamic and promising African investment landscape.

4

Chapter 4: Sectoral Opportunities in Africa

4.1: Agriculture and Agribusiness

As the morning sun painted the horizon with hues of orange and gold, Alex set out to explore the vast opportunities awaiting investors in Africa's agricultural sector. His first stop was a meeting with Dr. Fatima Diop, a leading expert in agricultural economics and agribusiness.

Dr. Diop welcomed Alex into her office, adorned with maps and charts depicting the agricultural landscape of Africa. "Good morning, Alex," she greeted him with a warm smile. "Today, we'll explore the immense potential of agriculture and agribusiness in Africa."

Alex settled into his chair, eager to learn from Dr. Diop's expertise. She began by highlighting the significance of agriculture in Africa's economy. "Agriculture is the backbone of many African economies, providing livelihoods for millions of people and contributing significantly to GDP," Dr. Diop explained. "With vast arable land, abundant water resources, and favorable climatic conditions, Africa has the potential to become a global powerhouse in agriculture."

She elaborated on the various opportunities available in the agricultural sector, ranging from crop production and livestock farming to agro-processing and value-added services. "Investors can capitalize on the growing demand for food and agricultural products in Africa and overseas," Dr. Diop said. "From small-scale farming to large commercial enterprises, there are opportunities for investors of all sizes to participate in Africa's agricultural transformation."

To provide a practical example, Dr. Diop arranged for Alex to visit a commercial farm in the fertile plains of Kenya. They toured the farm, witnessing firsthand the innovative farming practices and technologies being used to increase productivity and improve yields.

"As farmers, we have embraced modern agricultural techniques and technologies to maximize efficiency and profitability," the farm manager explained. "From precision farming and drip irrigation to greenhouse cultivation and crop rotation, we are constantly innovating to meet the growing demand for food."

As they delved deeper into the discussion, Dr. Diop highlighted the importance of value addition and agribusiness in unlocking the full potential of Africa's agricultural sector. "Agribusiness encompasses a wide range of activities, including processing, packaging, transportation, and marketing," she said. "Investors can add value to agricultural products and create employment opportunities along the value chain."

Later that afternoon, Dr. Diop arranged for Alex to attend

a seminar on agricultural investment opportunities in Africa. The event brought together farmers, agribusiness owners, policymakers, and investors to discuss best practices and emerging trends in the sector.

Alex found the seminar enlightening, gaining valuable insights into the vast opportunities available in Africa's agricultural sector. He was impressed by the level of innovation and entrepreneurship demonstrated by the speakers and participants.

As the day came to a close, Alex thanked Dr. Diop for her insights and guidance. He left her office feeling more enlightened about the immense potential of agriculture and agribusiness in Africa.

Back at his hotel, Alex reflected on the day's discussions. Agriculture and agribusiness offered promising opportunities for investors seeking to capitalize on Africa's agricultural potential. Armed with this knowledge, he felt better prepared to explore investment opportunities in the dynamic and evolving sector of African agriculture.

With a renewed sense of excitement, Alex prepared to continue his journey through Africa's investment landscape, knowing that agriculture and agribusiness would play a crucial role in driving economic growth and development across the continent.

4.2: Energy and Natural Resources

As the sun reached its zenith over the vast plains of Zambia, Alex embarked on the next leg of his journey to explore the abundant opportunities in Africa's energy and natural resources sector. His first destination was a meeting with Dr.

Kwame Nkrumah, a renowned expert in energy economics and resource management.

Dr. Nkrumah welcomed Alex into his office, adorned with maps and diagrams illustrating the rich tapestry of Africa's natural resources. "Good afternoon, Alex," he greeted him with a firm handshake. "Today, we'll delve into the immense potential of energy and natural resources in driving economic growth and development across Africa."

Alex settled into his chair, eager to learn from Dr. Nkrumah's expertise. He began by emphasizing the strategic importance of energy and natural resources in Africa's economy. "Africa is blessed with an abundance of natural resources, including oil, gas, minerals, and renewable energy sources," Dr. Nkrumah explained. "These resources are the foundation of many African economies, driving investment, employment, and infrastructure development."

He elaborated on the various opportunities available in the energy and natural resources sector, ranging from oil and gas exploration to mining, renewable energy, and conservation efforts. "Investors can capitalize on Africa's energy resources to meet the continent's growing energy needs and drive sustainable development," Dr. Nkrumah said. "From traditional fossil fuels to clean and renewable energy sources, there are opportunities for investors of all backgrounds to participate in Africa's energy transformation."

To provide a practical example, Dr. Nkrumah arranged for Alex to visit a solar power plant in the Kalahari Desert. They toured the facility, marveling at the vast arrays of solar panels harnessing the power of the sun to generate clean and sustainable energy.

"As the demand for energy continues to rise across Africa,

renewable energy sources such as solar, wind, and hydropower are becoming increasingly important," the plant manager explained. "Investing in renewable energy not only reduces carbon emissions and mitigates climate change but also creates jobs and promotes economic development."

As they delved deeper into the discussion, Dr. Nkrumah highlighted the importance of sustainable resource management and conservation efforts in Africa. "Natural resources such as minerals, forests, and water are essential for supporting livelihoods and driving economic growth," he said. "Investors must adopt responsible and sustainable practices to ensure the long-term viability of these resources for future generations."

Later that afternoon, Dr. Nkrumah arranged for Alex to attend a conference on energy and natural resources investment in Africa. The event brought together industry leaders, policymakers, and investors to discuss best practices and emerging trends in the sector.

Alex found the conference enlightening, gaining valuable insights into the vast opportunities available in Africa's energy and natural resources sector. He was impressed by the level of innovation and collaboration demonstrated by the speakers and participants.

As the day came to a close, Alex thanked Dr. Nkrumah for his insights and guidance. He left his office feeling more enlightened about the immense potential of energy and natural resources in Africa.

Back at his hotel, Alex reflected on the day's discussions. Energy and natural resources offered promising opportunities for investors seeking to contribute to Africa's development while generating returns on investment. Armed with this knowledge, he felt better prepared to explore investment opportunities in the dynamic and evolving sector of African energy and natural resources.

With a renewed sense of purpose, Alex prepared to continue his journey through Africa's investment landscape, knowing that energy and natural resources would play a crucial role in driving economic growth and development across the continent.

4.3: Technology and Telecommunications

As the city lights twinkled against the night sky of Nairobi, Alex's exploration of Africa's sectoral opportunities led him to the dynamic realm of technology and telecommunications. His next stop was a meeting with Dr. Aisha Malik, a leading expert in technology innovation and telecommunications infrastructure.

Dr. Malik welcomed Alex into her office, adorned with cutting-edge gadgets and futuristic prototypes. "Good evening, Alex," she greeted him with a warm smile. "Today, we'll explore the exciting possibilities unfolding in Africa's technology and telecommunications sector."

Alex settled into his chair, eager to learn from Dr. Malik's expertise. She began by highlighting the transformative impact of technology and telecommunications on Africa's economy. "Technology has the power to revolutionize industries, drive innovation, and improve the lives of millions of people across Africa," Dr. Malik explained. "From mobile banking and e-commerce to digital healthcare and smart cities, technology is reshaping the way we live, work, and interact."

She elaborated on the various opportunities available in the technology and telecommunications sector, ranging from software development and mobile applications to internet infrastructure and digital platforms. "Investors can capitalize on Africa's booming tech scene to drive economic growth and foster inclusive development," Dr. Malik said. "From startups and entrepreneurs to multinational corporations, there are opportunities for investors of all sizes to participate in Africa's digital revolution."

To provide a practical example, Dr. Malik arranged for Alex to visit a tech hub in the heart of Nairobi's innovation district. They toured the facility, witnessing firsthand the creativity and ingenuity of African entrepreneurs developing cutting-edge solutions to address local challenges.

"As tech entrepreneurs, we are harnessing the power of technology to drive social impact and economic empowerment," one entrepreneur explained. "From mobile payment platforms and agritech solutions to education apps and renewable energy innovations, African startups are leading the way in creating solutions that transform lives."

As they delved deeper into the discussion, Dr. Malik highlighted the importance of telecommunications infrastructure in enabling digital connectivity and access to information. "Telecommunications networks are the backbone of Africa's digital economy, providing essential services such as internet access, mobile connectivity, and digital communication," she said. "Investment in telecommunications infrastructure is essential for bridging the digital divide and unlocking the full potential of Africa's tech ecosystem."

Later that evening, Dr. Malik arranged for Alex to attend a conference on technology and telecommunications investment in Africa. The event brought together industry leaders, policymakers, and investors to discuss best practices and emerging trends in the sector.

Alex found the conference enlightening, gaining valuable insights into the vast opportunities available in Africa's technology and telecommunications sector. He was impressed by the level of innovation and collaboration demonstrated by the speakers and participants.

As the night came to a close, Alex thanked Dr. Malik for her insights and guidance. He left her office feeling more enlightened about the exciting possibilities unfolding in Africa's technology and telecommunications sector.

Back at his hotel, Alex reflected on the day's discussions. Technology and telecommunications offered promising opportunities for investors seeking to drive innovation and foster economic growth in Africa. Armed with this knowledge, he felt better prepared to explore investment opportunities in the dynamic and evolving sector of African technology and telecommunications.

With a renewed sense of excitement, Alex prepared to continue his journey through Africa's investment landscape, knowing that technology and telecommunications would play a crucial role in shaping the continent's future prosperity.

4.4: Infrastructure and Real Estate

As the sun rose over the sprawling cityscape of Johannesburg, Alex ventured into the realm of infrastructure and real estate, eager to explore the promising opportunities awaiting investors in Africa's burgeoning urban centers. His next destination was a meeting with Dr. Isabelle Mbeki, an esteemed expert in infrastructure development and real estate investment.

Dr. Mbeki welcomed Alex into her office, adorned with blueprints and models showcasing ambitious construction projects and urban developments. "Good morning, Alex," she greeted him with a warm smile. "Today, we'll delve into the exciting prospects unfolding in Africa's infrastructure and real estate sector."

Alex settled into his chair, ready to absorb Dr. Mbeki's insights. She began by emphasizing the critical role of infrastructure in driving economic growth and development across Africa. "Infrastructure is the backbone of modern societies, enabling the movement of goods and people, facilitating trade and commerce, and supporting urbanization and industrialization," Dr. Mbeki explained. "From transportation and energy to water and sanitation, Africa presents vast opportunities for infrastructure investment."

She elaborated on the various sectors within infrastructure and real estate, including transportation networks, energy utilities, telecommunications infrastructure, and commercial and residential developments. "Investors can capitalize on Africa's growing urbanization and expanding middle class to invest in infrastructure projects and real estate developments," Dr. Mbeki said. "From roads and railways to power plants and shopping malls, there are opportunities for investors to participate in projects that shape the future of Africa's cities."

To provide a practical example, Dr. Mbeki arranged for Alex to visit a construction site in the heart of Lagos, where a new metro line was under development. They toured the site, witnessing the bustling activity of engineers, architects, and laborers working together to bring the project to life.

"As developers, we are committed to building sustainable and inclusive urban environments that enhance quality of life

CHAPTER 4: SECTORAL OPPORTUNITIES IN AFRICA

and promote economic prosperity," the project manager explained. "Investment in infrastructure such as transportation networks not only improves connectivity and accessibility but also spurs economic growth and creates employment opportunities."

As they delved deeper into the discussion, Dr. Mbeki highlighted the importance of sustainable development practices and environmental considerations in infrastructure and real estate investments. "Investors must prioritize environmental sustainability and resilience in their projects to mitigate the impacts of climate change and promote long-term prosperity," she said. "From green building technologies to renewable energy solutions, there are opportunities for investors to integrate sustainability into their infrastructure and real estate projects."

Later that afternoon, Dr. Mbeki arranged for Alex to attend a conference on infrastructure and real estate investment in Africa. The event brought together industry leaders, policymakers, and investors to discuss best practices and emerging trends in the sector.

Alex found the conference enlightening, gaining valuable insights into the vast opportunities available in Africa's infrastructure and real estate sector. He was impressed by the level of innovation and collaboration demonstrated by the speakers and participants.

As the day came to a close, Alex thanked Dr. Mbeki for her insights and guidance. He left her office feeling more enlightened about the exciting prospects unfolding in Africa's infrastructure and real estate sector.

Back at his hotel, Alex reflected on the day's discussions. Infrastructure and real estate offered promising opportunities for investors seeking to drive economic growth and development in Africa's urban centers. Armed with this knowledge, he felt better prepared to explore investment opportunities in the dynamic and evolving sector of African infrastructure and real estate.

With a renewed sense of purpose, Alex prepared to continue his journey through Africa's investment landscape, knowing that infrastructure and real estate would play a crucial role in shaping the continent's future prosperity.

4.5: Financial Services

As the bustling streets of Accra came to life with the morning sun, Alex embarked on the exploration of another pivotal sector: financial services. His next rendezvous awaited him with Dr. Kwame Mensah, a distinguished figure in the realm of finance and banking.

Dr. Mensah welcomed Alex into his office, adorned with charts and graphs illustrating the intricate workings of financial markets. "Good morning, Alex," he greeted warmly. "Today, we'll uncover the vast opportunities within Africa's financial services sector."

Eagerly settling in, Alex listened as Dr. Mensah delved into the pivotal role of financial services in driving economic growth and empowering individuals and businesses across Africa. "Financial services form the backbone of Africa's economy, facilitating investment, savings, and entrepreneurship," Dr. Mensah explained. "From banking and insurance to capital markets and fintech, the financial sector offers a wide array of opportunities for investors seeking to participate in Africa's economic transformation."

He elucidated the various facets of financial services, highlighting the importance of inclusive banking, innovative fintech solutions, and robust regulatory frameworks. "Investors can leverage Africa's rapidly expanding middle class and increasing smartphone penetration to drive financial inclusion and innovation," Dr. Mensah said. "From mobile banking and digital payments to peer-to-peer lending and insurtech, there are opportunities for investors to capitalize on Africa's burgeoning fintech ecosystem."

To provide a tangible example, Dr. Mensah arranged for Alex to visit a bustling fintech hub in the heart of Nairobi. They toured the facility, witnessing the energy and creativity of entrepreneurs developing innovative financial solutions to address the needs of underserved communities.

"As fintech entrepreneurs, we are harnessing the power of technology to democratize access to financial services and drive inclusive economic growth," one entrepreneur explained. "From mobile money platforms and digital wallets to microfinance and blockchain-based solutions, African fintech startups are revolutionizing the way people save, borrow, and invest."

As they delved deeper into the discussion, Dr. Mensah emphasized the importance of robust regulatory frameworks and risk management practices in ensuring the stability and integrity of Africa's financial system. "Investors must prioritize transparency, accountability, and compliance in their operations to build trust and confidence among consumers and regulators," he said. "From anti-money laundering measures to consumer protection policies, responsible investing is essential for fostering a resilient and inclusive financial sector."

Later that afternoon, Dr. Mensah arranged for Alex to attend a conference on financial services innovation in Africa. The event brought together industry leaders, policymakers, and investors to discuss best practices and emerging trends in the sector.

Alex found the conference enlightening, gaining valuable insights into the vast opportunities available in Africa's financial services sector. He was impressed by the level of innovation and collaboration demonstrated by the speakers and participants.

As the day drew to a close, Alex thanked Dr. Mensah for his insights and guidance. He left his office feeling more enlightened about the exciting prospects within Africa's financial services sector.

Back at his hotel, Alex reflected on the day's discussions. Financial services offered promising opportunities for investors seeking to drive economic growth and empower individuals across Africa. Armed with this knowledge, he felt better prepared to explore investment opportunities in the dynamic and evolving sector of African financial services.

With a renewed sense of purpose, Alex prepared to continue his journey through Africa's investment landscape, knowing that financial services would play a crucial role in shaping the continent's future prosperity.

4.6: Healthcare and Pharmaceuticals

As the day unfolded in the vibrant city of Cape Town, Alex's exploration of Africa's sectoral opportunities led him to the critical realm of healthcare and pharmaceuticals. His next destination was a meeting with Dr. Fatima Abubakar, a distinguished expert in public health and pharmaceutical development.

Dr. Abubakar welcomed Alex into her office, adorned with medical journals and research papers showcasing the advancements in healthcare across Africa. "Good afternoon, Alex," she greeted him with a warm smile. "Today, we'll delve into the transformative potential of healthcare and pharmaceuticals in Africa."

Eager to learn, Alex settled into his chair as Dr. Abubakar began to elucidate the pivotal role of healthcare in driving economic development and improving quality of life across the continent. "Healthcare is a fundamental human right and a cornerstone of sustainable development," Dr. Abubakar explained. "From disease prevention and primary care to advanced medical treatments and pharmaceutical innovations, healthcare plays a crucial role in promoting well-being and productivity."

She elaborated on the various opportunities available in the healthcare and pharmaceutical sectors, ranging from investment in medical infrastructure and healthcare delivery systems to research and development of new drugs and medical technologies. "Investors can capitalize on Africa's growing healthcare market and rising demand for quality medical services and pharmaceutical products," Dr. Abubakar said. "From hospitals and clinics to pharmaceutical manufacturing facilities and research institutes, there are opportunities for investors to contribute to Africa's health sector transformation."

To provide a tangible example, Dr. Abubakar arranged for Alex to visit a state-of-the-art hospital in the heart of Johannesburg. They toured the facility, witnessing the cutting-edge medical equipment and innovative treatments being offered to patients.

"As healthcare providers, we are committed to delivering high-quality care and improving health outcomes for our communities," the hospital director explained. "Investment in medical infrastructure and technology is essential for expanding access to healthcare services and addressing the burden of disease across Africa."

As they delved deeper into the discussion, Dr. Abubakar emphasized the importance of pharmaceutical innovation in addressing Africa's healthcare challenges. "Pharmaceuticals play a crucial role in preventing and treating diseases, improving health outcomes, and enhancing quality of life," she said. "Investors can support the development and production of essential medicines and vaccines to address the unique health needs of African populations."

Later that afternoon, Dr. Abubakar arranged for Alex to attend a conference on healthcare innovation in Africa. The event brought together healthcare professionals, policymakers, and investors to discuss best practices and emerging trends in the sector.

Alex found the conference enlightening, gaining valuable insights into the vast opportunities available in Africa's healthcare and pharmaceutical sectors. He was impressed by the dedication and passion of the speakers and participants in improving healthcare access and outcomes across the continent.

As the day came to a close, Alex thanked Dr. Abubakar for her insights and guidance. He left her office feeling more enlightened about the transformative potential of healthcare and pharmaceuticals in Africa.

Back at his hotel, Alex reflected on the day's discussions. Healthcare and pharmaceuticals offered promising opportunities for investors seeking to make a meaningful impact on the well-being of African communities. Armed with this knowledge, he felt better prepared to explore investment opportunities in the dynamic and evolving sector of African healthcare and pharmaceuticals.

With a renewed sense of purpose, Alex prepared to continue his journey through Africa's investment landscape, knowing that healthcare and pharmaceuticals would play a crucial role in shaping the continent's future prosperity.

5

Chapter 5: Investing in Infrastructure

5.1: The Need for Infrastructure Development

As the sun rose over the vast plains of Africa, casting a golden glow on the horizon, Alex embarked on a new chapter of his exploration: investing in infrastructure. His first task was to understand the imperative need for infrastructure development across the continent. To gain insights, he arranged a meeting with Dr. Ahmed Suleiman, an esteemed economist specializing in infrastructure economics.

Dr. Suleiman welcomed Alex into his office, lined with books and maps detailing the infrastructure landscape of Africa. "Good morning, Alex," he greeted warmly. "Today, we'll delve into the critical importance of infrastructure development for Africa's economic growth and prosperity."

Eager to learn, Alex settled into his seat as Dr. Suleiman began to elucidate the significance of infrastructure. "Infrastructure serves as the backbone of any economy, facilitating trade, transportation, communication, and access to essential services," Dr. Suleiman explained. "From roads and railways to ports, airports, and energy networks, well-developed infrastructure is essential for driving economic development, reducing poverty, and improving quality of life."

He elaborated on the challenges facing Africa's infrastructure, including inadequate transportation networks, unreliable energy supply, and limited access to basic services such as water and sanitation. "Africa lags behind other regions in terms of infrastructure development, hindering its ability to compete in the global economy and meet the needs of its growing population," Dr. Suleiman said. "Investment in infrastructure is essential for unlocking Africa's potential and driving sustainable development."

To provide a tangible example, Dr. Suleiman arranged for Alex to visit a rural village in Tanzania, where access to clean water and electricity was limited. They met with community members who shared their struggles with accessing basic services and the impact it had on their daily lives.

"As a community, we face numerous challenges due to the lack of infrastructure," one villager explained. "Without access to clean water and electricity, we struggle to meet our basic needs and improve our standard of living."

As they delved deeper into the discussion, Dr. Suleiman emphasized the role of infrastructure in promoting economic growth, creating jobs, and reducing inequality. "Investment in infrastructure not only enhances productivity and competitiveness but also promotes social inclusion and resilience," he said. "From rural electrification projects to urban transport systems, infrastructure development has the power to transform lives and communities across Africa."

Later that afternoon, Dr. Suleiman arranged for Alex to

attend a conference on infrastructure investment in Africa. The event brought together policymakers, investors, and development partners to discuss strategies for addressing Africa's infrastructure challenges and unlocking investment opportunities.

Alex found the conference enlightening, gaining valuable insights into the urgent need for infrastructure development in Africa and the potential benefits of investment in this critical sector. He was inspired by the passion and commitment of the speakers and participants to drive positive change across the continent.

As the day drew to a close, Alex thanked Dr. Suleiman for his insights and guidance. He left his office feeling more determined than ever to contribute to Africa's infrastructure development and economic transformation.

Back at his hotel, Alex reflected on the day's discussions. Investing in infrastructure was not just about building roads and bridges; it was about creating opportunities, improving lives, and shaping the future of Africa. Armed with this understanding, he felt ready to embark on the next phase of his journey through Africa's investment landscape, knowing that infrastructure would be a key driver of progress and prosperity across the continent.

5.2: Transportation Networks

As the city bustled with activity under the midday sun, Alex delved deeper into the realm of infrastructure investment, focusing his attention on the critical importance of transportation networks in Africa's development. His next meeting was with Dr. Fatima Kamara, a renowned expert in transportation

CHAPTER 5: INVESTING IN INFRASTRUCTURE

economics and urban planning.

Dr. Kamara greeted Alex with a warm smile as he entered her office, adorned with maps and charts displaying the intricate web of transportation routes across Africa. "Good afternoon, Alex," she said. "Today, we'll explore the vital role of transportation networks in driving economic growth and connectivity."

Eager to learn, Alex took a seat as Dr. Kamara began to elucidate the significance of transportation infrastructure. "Transportation networks serve as the lifeblood of economies, facilitating the movement of goods, people, and services," she explained. "From roads and railways to ports and airports, well-developed transportation systems are essential for promoting trade, tourism, and investment."

She highlighted the challenges facing Africa's transportation networks, including inadequate road networks, limited railway connectivity, and congested urban areas. "Africa's transportation infrastructure lags behind other regions, hindering its ability to compete in the global market and realize its full economic potential," Dr. Kamara said. "Investment in transportation infrastructure is crucial for enhancing connectivity, reducing transportation costs, and promoting regional integration."

To provide a tangible example, Dr. Kamara arranged for Alex to visit a major port in Mombasa, Kenya, where goods from across the continent were being shipped and transported. They toured the port facilities, witnessing the bustling activity of cranes loading and unloading cargo from ships.

"As one of Africa's busiest ports, Mombasa plays a crucial role in facilitating trade and commerce across the region," the port manager explained. "Investment in port infrastructure is essential for increasing capacity, improving efficiency, and reducing logistics costs for businesses."

As they delved deeper into the discussion, Dr. Kamara emphasized the importance of sustainable transportation solutions in addressing Africa's development challenges. "Investors must prioritize environmentally friendly and inclusive transportation projects that promote economic growth and social equity," she said. "From public transportation systems to renewable energy-powered vehicles, there are opportunities to invest in innovative solutions that benefit both people and the planet."

Later that afternoon, Dr. Kamara arranged for Alex to attend a conference on transportation infrastructure investment in Africa. The event brought together policymakers, investors, and industry experts to discuss strategies for improving Africa's transportation networks and unlocking investment opportunities.

Alex found the conference enlightening, gaining valuable insights into the urgent need for investment in transportation infrastructure and the potential benefits of enhanced connectivity for Africa's economic development. He was inspired by the passion and commitment of the speakers and participants to drive positive change across the continent.

As the day came to a close, Alex thanked Dr. Kamara for her insights and guidance. He left her office feeling more determined than ever to contribute to Africa's transportation infrastructure development and economic transformation.

Back at his hotel, Alex reflected on the day's discussions. Transportation networks were the arteries of Africa's economy, connecting people, goods, and markets across vast distances. Armed with this understanding, he felt ready to explore investment opportunities that would not only generate returns but also make a meaningful impact on Africa's development journey.

5.3: Energy Infrastructure

As the sun dipped below the horizon, casting a warm glow over the city skyline, Alex continued his exploration of infrastructure investment, turning his attention to the critical need for energy infrastructure across Africa. His next meeting was with Dr. Jamal Mansour, an esteemed expert in energy economics and sustainable development.

Dr. Mansour welcomed Alex into his office, adorned with maps and diagrams illustrating the complex energy landscape of Africa. "Good evening, Alex," he greeted warmly. "Today, we'll delve into the vital role of energy infrastructure in powering Africa's economic growth and development."

Eager to learn, Alex settled into his seat as Dr. Mansour began to elucidate the significance of energy infrastructure. "Energy is the lifeblood of modern economies, driving industrialization, powering households, and fueling economic activity," Dr. Mansour explained. "From electricity generation and transmission to oil and gas pipelines, well-developed energy infrastructure is essential for promoting economic growth, enhancing quality of life, and reducing poverty."

He highlighted the challenges facing Africa's energy sector, including limited access to electricity, unreliable energy supply, and dependence on fossil fuels. "Africa's energy infrastructure lags behind other regions, hindering its ability to meet the growing energy demand and transition to a sustainable energy future," Dr. Mansour said. "Investment in energy infrastructure is crucial for expanding access to electricity, promoting renewable energy, and addressing climate change."

To provide a tangible example, Dr. Mansour arranged for Alex to visit a solar power plant in the Sahel region, where the sun's rays were harnessed to generate clean and renewable energy. They toured the plant, witnessing rows of solar panels stretching across the desert landscape.

"As one of Africa's largest solar power plants, this facility plays a crucial role in providing clean and reliable electricity to communities across the region," the plant manager explained. "Investment in renewable energy infrastructure is essential for reducing carbon emissions, mitigating climate change, and promoting sustainable development."

As they delved deeper into the discussion, Dr. Mansour emphasized the importance of inclusive energy solutions in addressing Africa's development challenges. "Investors must prioritize projects that benefit both urban and rural communities, promote energy efficiency, and empower local communities," he said. "From off-grid solar systems to mini-grids and energy-efficient technologies, there are opportunities to invest in innovative solutions that expand energy access and promote social equity."

Later that evening, Dr. Mansour arranged for Alex to attend a conference on energy infrastructure investment in Africa. The event brought together policymakers, investors, and energy experts to discuss strategies for improving Africa's energy infrastructure and unlocking investment opportunities.

Alex found the conference enlightening, gaining valuable insights into the urgent need for investment in energy infrastructure and the potential benefits of renewable energy for Africa's economic development. He was inspired by the passion and commitment of the speakers and participants to drive positive change across the continent.

As the night came to a close, Alex thanked Dr. Mansour for his insights and guidance. He left his office feeling more determined than ever to contribute to Africa's energy infrastructure development and transition to a sustainable energy future.

Back at his hotel, Alex reflected on the day's discussions. Energy infrastructure was the backbone of Africa's development, powering progress and prosperity across the continent. Armed with this understanding, he felt ready to explore investment opportunities that would not only generate returns but also make a meaningful impact on Africa's energy transition and sustainable development journey.

5.4: Water and Sanitation Projects

As dawn broke over the sprawling landscape, Alex's journey into infrastructure investment led him to explore the critical realm of water and sanitation projects in Africa. His next meeting awaited him with Dr. Amina Diop, a leading expert in water resource management and sanitation infrastructure.

Dr. Diop greeted Alex with a warm smile as he entered her office, adorned with maps and charts illustrating the challenges and opportunities in Africa's water sector. "Good morning, Alex," she said. "Today, we'll delve into the essential role of water and sanitation projects in promoting health, hygiene, and sustainable development."

Eager to learn, Alex took a seat as Dr. Diop began to elucidate the significance of water infrastructure. "Access to clean water and sanitation is a basic human right and a fundamental prerequisite for health, dignity, and economic development," Dr. Diop explained. "From drinking water supply systems to wastewater treatment plants and sanitation facilities, well-developed water infrastructure is essential for improving public health, protecting the environment, and enhancing quality of life."

She highlighted the challenges facing Africa's water sector, including limited access to clean water, inadequate sanitation facilities, and water scarcity exacerbated by climate change. "Many communities across Africa lack access to safe and reliable water sources, leading to waterborne diseases and environmental degradation," Dr. Diop said. "Investment in water and sanitation projects is crucial for expanding access to clean water, promoting hygiene practices, and ensuring environmental sustainability."

To provide a tangible example, Dr. Diop arranged for Alex to visit a rural village in Ghana, where a community-led water project was underway. They met with local leaders and community members who shared their experiences with water scarcity and the impact it had on their daily lives.

"As a community, we face numerous challenges due to the lack of access to clean water," one villager explained. "With the support of this water project, we are working together to dig wells, install water pumps, and build latrines to improve sanitation and hygiene in our village."

As they delved deeper into the discussion, Dr. Diop emphasized the importance of sustainable water management practices in addressing Africa's water challenges. "Investors must prioritize projects that promote water conservation, watershed management, and climate resilience," she said. "From rainwater harvesting systems to water reuse technologies,

CHAPTER 5: INVESTING IN INFRASTRUCTURE

there are opportunities to invest in innovative solutions that enhance water security and build community resilience."

Later that afternoon, Dr. Diop arranged for Alex to attend a conference on water and sanitation investment in Africa. The event brought together policymakers, investors, and water experts to discuss strategies for improving access to clean water and sanitation services and unlocking investment opportunities.

Alex found the conference enlightening, gaining valuable insights into the urgent need for investment in water and sanitation projects and the potential benefits for Africa's health, environment, and economy. He was inspired by the dedication and commitment of the speakers and participants to address Africa's water challenges and improve the lives of millions of people across the continent.

As the day came to a close, Alex thanked Dr. Diop for her insights and guidance. He left her office feeling more determined than ever to contribute to Africa's water and sanitation infrastructure development and sustainable development journey.

Back at his hotel, Alex reflected on the day's discussions. Water and sanitation projects were essential for promoting health, dignity, and economic development in Africa. Armed with this understanding, he felt ready to explore investment opportunities that would not only generate returns but also make a meaningful impact on Africa's water security and public health.

5.5: Public-Private Partnerships

As the day progressed, Alex's exploration of infrastructure investment led him to delve into the crucial realm of public-private partnerships (PPPs) in Africa. His next meeting awaited him with Mr. Joseph Okon, an experienced expert in infrastructure finance and PPPs.

Mr. Okon welcomed Alex into his office, adorned with charts and diagrams illustrating successful PPP projects across Africa. "Good afternoon, Alex," he greeted warmly. "Today, we'll delve into the transformative potential of public-private partnerships in addressing Africa's infrastructure needs."

Eager to learn, Alex settled into his seat as Mr. Okon began to elucidate the significance of PPPs. "Public-private partnerships are collaborative arrangements between government agencies and private sector entities to develop, finance, and operate infrastructure projects," Mr. Okon explained. "From transportation and energy to water and telecommunications, PPPs offer a flexible and efficient mechanism for mobilizing private capital and expertise to address Africa's infrastructure challenges."

He highlighted the benefits of PPPs, including increased efficiency, reduced government fiscal burden, and improved service delivery. "PPPs can leverage the strengths of both the public and private sectors to deliver infrastructure projects that meet the needs of communities and contribute to economic growth and development," Mr. Okon said. "By sharing risks and responsibilities, PPPs can unlock investment, promote innovation, and ensure the long-term sustainability of infrastructure assets."

To provide a tangible example, Mr. Okon arranged for Alex

to visit a PPP project in Nigeria, where a private consortium had partnered with the government to develop a toll road network. They toured the highway, witnessing the seamless flow of traffic and the modern infrastructure provided by the PPP.

"As a PPP project, this toll road network has significantly reduced travel times, improved road safety, and stimulated economic activity along the corridor," the project manager explained. "By combining public resources with private sector expertise, we were able to deliver this vital infrastructure project on time and within budget."

As they delved deeper into the discussion, Mr. Okon emphasized the importance of a transparent and robust regulatory framework in facilitating successful PPPs. "Effective governance, clear legal frameworks, and transparent procurement processes are essential for attracting private investment and ensuring the success of PPP projects," he said. "Investors must have confidence in the regulatory environment and the stability of contractual arrangements to commit long-term capital to infrastructure projects."

Later that afternoon, Mr. Okon arranged for Alex to attend a conference on infrastructure financing and PPPs in Africa. The event brought together government officials, private sector representatives, and financiers to discuss best practices and emerging trends in PPP implementation.

Alex found the conference enlightening, gaining valuable insights into the role of PPPs in addressing Africa's infrastructure needs and unlocking investment opportunities. He was impressed by the collaborative spirit and innovative approaches showcased by the speakers and participants.

As the day came to a close, Alex thanked Mr. Okon for his

insights and guidance. He left his office feeling more determined than ever to explore opportunities for infrastructure investment through public-private partnerships.

Back at his hotel, Alex reflected on the day's discussions. Public-private partnerships offered a promising avenue for mobilizing private capital and expertise to address Africa's infrastructure challenges. Armed with this understanding, he felt ready to pursue investment opportunities that would not only generate returns but also contribute to the sustainable development and prosperity of Africa.

5.6: Summary and Conclusion

As the day drew to a close, Alex reflected on the wealth of knowledge he had gained during his exploration of infrastructure investment in Africa. His meeting with various experts and visits to infrastructure projects had provided him with valuable insights into the critical role of infrastructure in driving economic growth and development across the continent.

In his final meeting of the day, Alex sat down with Dr. Evelyn Ngugi, a seasoned economist specializing in infrastructure investment. Dr. Ngugi welcomed Alex warmly and began to summarize the key takeaways from their discussions.

"Alex, throughout our exploration of infrastructure investment, we have learned that infrastructure is the backbone of economic development in Africa," Dr. Ngugi began. "From transportation and energy to water and sanitation, well-developed infrastructure is essential for promoting trade, improving access to essential services, and enhancing quality of life."

She highlighted the urgent need for investment in infrastructure to address Africa's development challenges and unlock its full potential. "Africa faces numerous infrastructure deficits, including inadequate transportation networks, unreliable energy supply, and limited access to clean water and sanitation," Dr. Ngugi said. "Investment in infrastructure is crucial for bridging these gaps, promoting inclusive growth, and building a resilient and sustainable future for the continent."

Dr. Ngugi emphasized the importance of innovative financing mechanisms, such as public-private partnerships, in mobilizing private capital and expertise to address Africa's infrastructure needs. "Public-private partnerships offer a flexible and efficient mechanism for delivering infrastructure projects that meet the needs of communities and contribute to economic development," she said. "By leveraging the strengths of both the public and private sectors, PPPs can drive innovation, improve service delivery, and ensure the long-term sustainability of infrastructure assets."

As their meeting came to a close, Dr. Ngugi thanked Alex for his engagement and commitment to understanding the complexities of infrastructure investment in Africa. "I hope our discussions have provided you with valuable insights into the transformative potential of infrastructure investment," she said. "By investing in infrastructure, you have the opportunity to not only generate financial returns but also make a meaningful impact on the lives of millions of people across the continent."

As Alex left Dr. Ngugi's office, he felt a sense of purpose and determination. Infrastructure investment was not just about building roads and bridges; it was about unlocking Africa's potential, driving economic growth, and improving the lives of millions of people. Armed with this newfound knowledge, Alex was ready to embark on his journey as an infrastructure investor, knowing that his efforts would contribute to the sustainable development and prosperity of Africa.

Back at his hotel, Alex reflected on the day's discussions. Investing in infrastructure was not without its challenges, but the potential rewards were immense. With a renewed sense of purpose and determination, Alex prepared to continue his journey through Africa's investment landscape, knowing that infrastructure would play a crucial role in shaping the continent's future prosperity.

6

Chapter 6: The Role of Technology and Innovation

6.1: Digital Transformation in Africa

As the sun rose over the bustling city skyline, Alex embarked on a new chapter of his exploration: the transformative role of technology and innovation in Africa. His first meeting of the day was with Dr. Ngozi Okafor, a renowned expert in digital transformation and technology innovation.

Dr. Okafor greeted Alex with a warm smile as he entered her office, adorned with sleek gadgets and futuristic prototypes. "Good morning, Alex," she said. "Today, we'll delve into the exciting world of digital transformation and its impact on Africa's development."

Eager to learn, Alex settled into his seat as Dr. Okafor began to elucidate the significance of digital transformation. "Digital technology has the power to revolutionize economies, societies, and industries, enabling innovation, driving efficiency, and expanding opportunities," Dr. Okafor explained. "From mobile phones and internet connectivity to e-commerce platforms and digital payments, digital transformation is reshaping the way Africans live, work, and interact."

She highlighted the challenges facing Africa's digital transformation, including limited access to affordable internet, inadequate digital infrastructure, and a digital skills gap. "Africa has made significant strides in recent years in terms of digital adoption, but there is still much work to be done to ensure that all Africans can benefit from the opportunities presented by digital technology," Dr. Okafor said. "Investment in digital infrastructure, skills development, and regulatory frameworks is essential for accelerating digital transformation and unlocking its full potential."

To provide a tangible example, Dr. Okafor arranged for Alex to visit a technology hub in Lagos, Nigeria, where young entrepreneurs were developing innovative solutions to address local challenges. They toured the facility, witnessing the energy and creativity of the startups as they pitched their ideas and prototypes.

"As entrepreneurs, we are harnessing the power of technology to solve some of Africa's most pressing problems," one entrepreneur explained. "From fintech and agritech to healthtech and edtech, African startups are leading the way in innovation and entrepreneurship."

As they delved deeper into the discussion, Dr. Okafor emphasized the importance of collaboration and partnership in driving Africa's digital transformation. "Governments, businesses, and civil society must work together to create an enabling environment for digital innovation and entrepreneurship to thrive," she said. "From supportive policies and regulations to investment in digital infrastructure and education, there are opportunities for all stakeholders to contribute to Africa's digital future."

Later that afternoon, Dr. Okafor arranged for Alex to attend a conference on digital transformation in Africa. The event brought together policymakers, technology experts, and entrepreneurs to discuss best practices and emerging trends in digital innovation.

Alex found the conference enlightening, gaining valuable insights into the transformative potential of digital technology and innovation in Africa. He was inspired by the passion and creativity of the speakers and participants in leveraging technology to drive positive change across the continent.

As the day came to a close, Alex thanked Dr. Okafor for her insights and guidance. He left her office feeling more determined than ever to explore opportunities for investment in digital transformation and technology innovation in Africa.

Back at his hotel, Alex reflected on the day's discussions. Digital transformation was not just about adopting new technologies; it was about harnessing the power of innovation to address Africa's development challenges and unlock its full potential. Armed with this understanding, he felt ready to embark on the next phase of his journey through Africa's investment landscape, knowing that technology and innovation would play a crucial role in shaping the continent's future prosperity.

6.2: Fintech and Financial Inclusion

As the city buzzed with energy under the midday sun, Alex delved deeper into the transformative role of technology and innovation in Africa, focusing his attention on the burgeoning field of fintech and its impact on financial inclusion. His next meeting was with Ms. Fatima Nkosi, a leading expert in fintech and financial services.

Ms. Nkosi greeted Alex with a warm smile as he entered her office, adorned with charts and graphs illustrating the growth of fintech in Africa. "Good afternoon, Alex," she said. "Today, we'll explore the exciting world of fintech and its potential to promote financial inclusion and empower communities across the continent."

Eager to learn, Alex settled into his seat as Ms. Nkosi began to elucidate the significance of fintech. "Fintech refers to the use of technology to deliver financial services, such as banking, payments, and lending, in innovative and efficient ways," she explained. "From mobile money and digital banking to peer-to-peer lending and crowdfunding, fintech is revolutionizing the way Africans access and manage their finances."

She highlighted the challenges facing financial inclusion in Africa, including limited access to formal banking services, high transaction costs, and a lack of financial literacy. "Millions of Africans remain excluded from the formal financial system, limiting their ability to save, borrow, and invest in their futures," Ms. Nkosi said. "Fintech offers a promising solution to these challenges by providing accessible, affordable, and convenient financial services to underserved populations."

To provide a tangible example, Ms. Nkosi arranged for Alex to visit a fintech startup in Nairobi, Kenya, where innovative mobile banking solutions were transforming the way people managed their money. They met with the founders, who explained how their mobile app was enabling users to save, borrow, and invest with ease.

"As a fintech company, we are committed to promoting financial inclusion and empowering individuals to take control of their financial futures," one founder explained. "Through our mobile banking platform, we are breaking down barriers to access and providing affordable financial services to millions of people across Africa."

As they delved deeper into the discussion, Ms. Nkosi emphasized the importance of collaboration and innovation in driving fintech's growth and impact in Africa. "Governments, regulators, and financial institutions must work together with fintech startups to create an enabling environment for innovation and entrepreneurship to thrive," she said. "From supportive policies and regulations to investment in digital infrastructure and financial education, there are opportunities for all stakeholders to contribute to expanding financial inclusion and promoting economic empowerment."

Later that afternoon, Ms. Nkosi arranged for Alex to attend a conference on fintech and financial inclusion in Africa. The event brought together industry leaders, policymakers, and fintech innovators to discuss strategies for harnessing technology to promote financial inclusion and empower communities.

Alex found the conference enlightening, gaining valuable insights into the transformative potential of fintech in Africa. He was inspired by the passion and commitment of the speakers and participants in leveraging technology to create a more inclusive and equitable financial system across the continent.

As the day came to a close, Alex thanked Ms. Nkosi for her insights and guidance. He left her office feeling more determined than ever to explore opportunities for investment in fintech and financial inclusion in Africa.

Back at his hotel, Alex reflected on the day's discussions. Fintech was not just about innovation; it was about empowering individuals, transforming communities, and driving economic growth. Armed with this understanding, he felt ready to pursue investment opportunities that would not only generate returns but also make a meaningful impact on the lives of millions of people across Africa.

6.3: Tech Hubs and Startups

As the sun set over the vibrant cityscape, Alex continued his exploration of technology and innovation in Africa, shifting his focus to the dynamic ecosystem of tech hubs and startups driving entrepreneurial growth. His next meeting awaited him with Mr. Kwame Asante, a visionary entrepreneur and founder of one of Africa's leading tech hubs.

Mr. Asante welcomed Alex with a firm handshake as he entered the bustling hub, alive with the hum of creativity and innovation. "Good evening, Alex," he greeted warmly. "Today, we'll dive into the exciting world of tech hubs and startups and their role in shaping Africa's digital future."

Eager to learn, Alex took a seat as Mr. Asante began to elucidate the significance of tech hubs. "Tech hubs serve as catalysts for innovation and entrepreneurship, providing a supportive environment for startups to thrive and grow," he explained. "From co-working spaces and incubator programs to mentorship and networking opportunities, tech hubs offer a range of resources and support services to help startups overcome challenges and scale their businesses."

He highlighted the challenges facing startups in Africa, including limited access to funding, a shortage of technical talent, and a lack of supportive ecosystems. "Despite these challenges, African startups are thriving, leveraging technology to address local problems and unlock new opportunities," Mr. Asante said. "Tech hubs play a crucial role in nurturing this entrepreneurial talent and building vibrant startup ecosystems across the continent."

To provide a tangible example, Mr. Asante arranged for Alex to tour the tech hub and meet with some of the startups based there. They visited bustling workspaces, where teams of developers and entrepreneurs were hard at work on their latest projects.

"As a startup founder, being part of this tech hub has been instrumental in our success," one entrepreneur explained. "The support, mentorship, and collaboration opportunities provided here have helped us grow our business and access new markets."

As they delved deeper into the discussion, Mr. Asante emphasized the importance of collaboration and community in driving innovation and entrepreneurship. "Tech hubs bring together diverse talent and ideas, fostering creativity, collaboration, and knowledge sharing," he said. "By creating a supportive ecosystem for startups to thrive, tech hubs are driving economic growth, creating jobs, and catalyzing social change across Africa."

Later that evening, Mr. Asante arranged for Alex to attend a pitch competition at the tech hub, where startups showcased their innovative solutions to a panel of investors and industry experts.

Alex found the competition exhilarating, witnessing firsthand the creativity and ingenuity of African startups in solving local challenges and driving innovation. He was inspired by the passion and determination of the entrepreneurs and the supportive community fostered by the tech hub.

As the night came to a close, Alex thanked Mr. Asante for his insights and hospitality. He left the tech hub feeling energized and inspired, eager to explore opportunities for investment in Africa's vibrant startup ecosystem.

Back at his hotel, Alex reflected on the day's discussions. Tech hubs and startups were at the forefront of Africa's digital transformation, driving innovation, creating jobs, and unlocking new opportunities across the continent. Armed with this understanding, he felt ready to pursue investment opportunities that would not only generate returns but also support the growth and success of Africa's entrepreneurial ecosystem.

6.4: E-Commerce and Mobile Payments

As the city lights glimmered in the night, Alex delved deeper into the realm of technology and innovation, exploring the transformative impact of e-commerce and mobile payments in Africa. His next meeting awaited him with Ms. Aisha Kamara, a leading expert in digital commerce and mobile finance.

Ms. Kamara welcomed Alex with a warm smile as he entered her office, adorned with charts and graphs showcasing the exponential growth of e-commerce and mobile payments in Africa. "Good evening, Alex," she said. "Today, we'll delve into the exciting world of e-commerce and mobile payments and their role in revolutionizing Africa's retail landscape."

Eager to learn, Alex settled into his seat as Ms. Kamara began to elucidate the significance of e-commerce. "E-commerce refers to the buying and selling of goods and services over the internet, providing consumers with access to a wide range of products and services from the comfort of their homes," she explained. "From online marketplaces and digital storefronts to payment gateways and delivery services, e-commerce is transforming the way Africans shop and do business."

She highlighted the challenges facing traditional retail in Africa, including limited access to formal retail outlets, high transaction costs, and logistical challenges. "E-commerce offers a solution to these challenges by providing a convenient and accessible platform for consumers to purchase goods and services," Ms. Kamara said. "From groceries and clothing to electronics and household goods, e-commerce platforms are catering to the diverse needs and preferences of African consumers."

To provide a tangible example, Ms. Kamara arranged for Alex to visit a bustling marketplace in Accra, Ghana, where vendors were selling their products online through a popular e-commerce platform. They toured the marketplace, witnessing the seamless integration of online and offline retail experiences.

"As a small business owner, e-commerce has transformed my business, enabling me to reach customers beyond my local market and expand my sales," one vendor explained. "Through the e-commerce platform, I can showcase my products, process payments, and arrange for delivery to customers' doorsteps, all with just a few clicks."

As they delved deeper into the discussion, Ms. Kamara emphasized the importance of mobile payments in driving the growth of e-commerce in Africa. "Mobile payments allow consumers to make secure and convenient transactions using their mobile phones, reducing the reliance on cash and traditional banking services," she said. "From mobile wallets and payment apps to USSD codes and QR code payments, mobile payments are empowering millions of Africans to participate in the digital economy."

Later that evening, Ms. Kamara arranged for Alex to attend a seminar on e-commerce and mobile payments in Africa. The event brought together entrepreneurs, retailers, and fintech companies to discuss strategies for leveraging technology to drive growth and innovation in the retail sector.

Alex found the seminar enlightening, gaining valuable insights into the transformative potential of e-commerce and mobile payments in Africa. He was impressed by the diversity of businesses and the entrepreneurial spirit driving innovation in the retail sector.

As the night came to a close, Alex thanked Ms. Kamara for her insights and hospitality. He left her office feeling inspired and energized, eager to explore opportunities for investment in Africa's booming e-commerce and mobile payments industry.

Back at his hotel, Alex reflected on the day's discussions. E-commerce and mobile payments were revolutionizing Africa's retail landscape, creating new opportunities for businesses and consumers alike. Armed with this understanding, he felt ready to pursue investment opportunities that would not only generate returns but also contribute to the growth and prosperity of Africa's digital economy.

6.5: Opportunities in ICT Infrastructure

As the moon illuminated the cityscape, Alex delved further into the realm of technology and innovation, exploring the vast opportunities presented by Information and Communication Technology (ICT) infrastructure in Africa. His next meeting awaited him with Mr. Ahmed Abubakar, a seasoned expert in telecommunications and ICT infrastructure development.

Mr. Abubakar welcomed Alex into his office, adorned with maps and blueprints illustrating the intricate network of telecommunications infrastructure across Africa. "Good evening, Alex," he greeted warmly. "Today, we'll explore the exciting world of ICT infrastructure and the opportunities it presents for driving economic growth and development."

Eager to learn, Alex settled into his seat as Mr. Abubakar began to elucidate the significance of ICT infrastructure. "ICT infrastructure encompasses the physical and virtual components that enable the transmission, processing, and storage of information," he explained. "From fiber optic cables and mobile networks to data centers and cloud computing services, ICT infrastructure forms the backbone of the digital economy and underpins innovation and connectivity."

He highlighted the challenges facing ICT infrastructure development in Africa, including limited access to high-speed internet, inadequate digital literacy, and regulatory barriers. "Despite these challenges, Africa has made significant progress in recent years in expanding ICT infrastructure and increasing internet penetration," Mr. Abubakar said. "Investment in ICT infrastructure is essential for bridging the digital divide, promoting digital inclusion, and unlocking new opportunities for economic growth and development."

To provide a tangible example, Mr. Abubakar arranged for Alex to visit a telecommunications hub in Nairobi, Kenya, where the latest technology was powering connectivity across the region. They toured the facility, witnessing the intricate network of fiber optic cables and state-of-the-art equipment that formed the backbone of the telecommunications infrastructure.

"As a telecommunications provider, we are committed to expanding access to high-speed internet and digital services across Africa," one engineer explained. "Through investments in ICT infrastructure, we are connecting communities, empowering businesses, and driving innovation across the continent."

As they delved deeper into the discussion, Mr. Abubakar emphasized the importance of collaboration and innovation in driving ICT infrastructure development. "Governments, regulators, and private sector stakeholders must work together to create an enabling environment for investment in ICT infrastructure," he said. "From supportive policies and regulations to public-private partnerships and investment incentives, there are opportunities to accelerate the expansion of ICT infrastructure and unlock its full potential for Africa's development."

Later that evening, Mr. Abubakar arranged for Alex to attend a forum on ICT infrastructure investment in Africa. The event brought together industry leaders, policymakers, and investors to discuss strategies for expanding access to high-speed internet and digital services across the continent.

Alex found the forum enlightening, gaining valuable insights into the transformative potential of ICT infrastructure in Africa. He was inspired by the vision and commitment of the speakers and participants in harnessing technology to drive economic growth and development across the continent.

As the night came to a close, Alex thanked Mr. Abubakar for his insights and guidance. He left his office feeling more determined than ever to explore opportunities for investment in ICT infrastructure in Africa.

Back at his hotel, Alex reflected on the day's discussions. ICT infrastructure was the foundation of Africa's digital future, unlocking new opportunities for innovation, connectivity, and prosperity. Armed with this understanding, he felt ready to pursue investment opportunities that would not only generate returns but also contribute to the growth and development of Africa's digital economy.

6.6: Summary and Conclusion

As the night grew deeper, Alex wrapped up his exploration of technology and innovation in Africa, reflecting on the transformative potential of ICT infrastructure, e-commerce, fintech, and more. His final meeting of the day was with Dr. Sarah Mensah, a renowned thought leader in the field of technology and innovation.

Dr. Mensah welcomed Alex into her office, a sanctuary of knowledge adorned with books and digital displays showcasing the latest advancements in technology. "Good evening, Alex," she greeted warmly. "Today, we've embarked on a journey through the world of technology and innovation in Africa, exploring the opportunities and challenges that lie ahead."

Eager to summarize their discussions, Dr. Mensah began to elucidate the key takeaways from their exploration. "Throughout our journey, we've seen how technology and innovation are reshaping Africa's economy, society, and future," she said. "From ICT infrastructure and e-commerce to fintech and startup ecosystems, Africa is harnessing the power of technology to drive inclusive growth, create jobs, and improve lives."

She highlighted the challenges facing Africa's technology and innovation landscape, including limited access to infrastructure, digital skills gaps, and regulatory barriers. "Despite these challenges, Africa has demonstrated remarkable resilience and creativity in leveraging technology to address local challenges and unlock new opportunities," Dr. Mensah said. "Investment in technology and innovation is essential for driving Africa's development agenda and ensuring that no one is left behind in the digital revolution."

To provide a final reflection, Dr. Mensah emphasized the importance of collaboration, partnership, and innovation in shaping Africa's digital future. "Governments, businesses, civil society, and international partners must work together to create an enabling environment for technology and innovation to thrive," she said. "From supportive policies and regulations to investments in infrastructure, education, and research, there are opportunities for all stakeholders to contribute to Africa's digital transformation journey."

As their meeting came to a close, Dr. Mensah thanked Alex for his engagement and curiosity throughout their discussions. "I hope our journey has provided you with valuable insights into the exciting opportunities and challenges of technology and innovation in Africa," she said. "By investing in technology and innovation, you have the opportunity to not only generate financial returns but also make a meaningful impact on the lives of millions of people across the continent."

Alex left Dr. Mensah's office feeling inspired and enlightened by their conversation. Technology and innovation were not just buzzwords; they were catalysts for change, driving progress and prosperity across Africa. Armed with a deeper understanding of the role of technology in Africa's development, Alex felt ready to embark on his journey as an investor, knowing that his contributions would help shape Africa's digital future.

As he stepped out into the cool night air, Alex gazed up at the stars, filled with hope and excitement for the possibilities that lay ahead. Africa's technology and innovation landscape was vast and dynamic, and he was ready to be a part of it, making a difference one investment at a time.

Chapter 7: Agricultural Investment Opportunities

7.1: The Importance of Agriculture in Africa

As the sun rose over the vast savannah, Alex embarked on a new chapter of his exploration: agricultural investment opportunities in Africa. His journey began with a meeting with Dr. Fatima Diop, a renowned agricultural economist and advocate for rural development.

Dr. Diop welcomed Alex into her office, adorned with maps and charts depicting the agricultural landscape of Africa. "Good morning, Alex," she greeted warmly. "Today, we'll delve into the importance of agriculture in Africa and the opportunities it presents for investment and development."

Eager to learn, Alex settled into his seat as Dr. Diop began to elucidate the significance of agriculture. "Agriculture is the backbone of Africa's economy, employing the majority of the continent's workforce and contributing significantly to GDP," she explained. "From smallholder farmers and agribusinesses to large-scale commercial operations, agriculture plays a crucial role in providing food security, generating income, and driving rural development across Africa."

She highlighted the challenges facing agriculture in Africa, including climate change, land degradation, and limited access to markets and finance. "Despite these challenges, Africa has immense agricultural potential, with vast arable land, abundant water resources, and a rich diversity of crops and livestock," Dr. Diop said. "Investment in agriculture is essential for unlocking this potential, improving productivity, and ensuring the sustainability of food production systems."

To provide a tangible example, Dr. Diop arranged for Alex to visit a rural farming community in Tanzania, where smallholder farmers were working the land with traditional methods. They toured the fields, witnessing the hard work and dedication of the farmers as they tended to their crops.

"As a smallholder farmer, agriculture is not just a livelihood; it's a way of life," one farmer explained. "Through investment in technology, training, and access to markets, we can improve our yields, increase our incomes, and build a better future for our families and communities."

As they delved deeper into the discussion, Dr. Diop emphasized the importance of sustainable agriculture in Africa's development. "Sustainable agriculture practices, such as conservation agriculture and agroforestry, are essential for preserving natural resources, mitigating climate change, and ensuring the long-term viability of food production systems," she said. "Investment in sustainable agriculture is not only good for the environment but also essential for building resilient and inclusive food systems that can withstand future shocks and challenges."

Later that afternoon, Dr. Diop arranged for Alex to attend a conference on agricultural investment in Africa. The event brought together policymakers, investors, and development partners to discuss strategies for promoting sustainable agriculture and rural development across the continent.

Alex found the conference enlightening, gaining valuable insights into the importance of agriculture in Africa's development and the opportunities it presents for investment and growth. He was inspired by the passion and commitment of the speakers and participants in addressing the challenges facing agriculture and unlocking its potential to drive economic transformation and improve livelihoods across the continent.

As the day came to a close, Alex thanked Dr. Diop for her insights and hospitality. He left her office feeling more determined than ever to explore opportunities for investment in agriculture in Africa.

Back at his hotel, Alex reflected on the day's discussions. Agriculture was not just about farming; it was about feeding communities, creating livelihoods, and driving economic development. Armed with this understanding, he felt ready to pursue investment opportunities that would not only generate returns but also make a meaningful impact on the lives of millions of people across Africa.

7.2: Agribusiness Value Chains

As the morning sun cast a golden hue over the fields, Alex continued his exploration of agricultural investment opportunities in Africa, focusing his attention on the intricate web of agribusiness value chains. His next meeting awaited him with Mr. Kwame Mensah, a seasoned entrepreneur and advocate

CHAPTER 7: AGRICULTURAL INVESTMENT OPPORTUNITIES

for agricultural value addition.

Mr. Mensah welcomed Alex into his office, adorned with posters depicting the various stages of the agricultural value chain, from farm to fork. "Good morning, Alex," he greeted warmly. "Today, we'll delve into the world of agribusiness value chains and the opportunities they present for investment and growth."

Eager to learn, Alex settled into his seat as Mr. Mensah began to elucidate the significance of agribusiness value chains. "Agribusiness value chains encompass the full range of activities involved in bringing agricultural products from the farm to the consumer," he explained. "From production and processing to distribution and marketing, agribusiness value chains play a crucial role in adding value to agricultural products and connecting farmers to markets."

He highlighted the challenges facing agribusiness value chains in Africa, including inadequate infrastructure, limited access to finance, and fragmented markets. "Despite these challenges, Africa has immense potential to develop vibrant and sustainable agribusiness value chains," Mr. Mensah said. "Investment in infrastructure, technology, and market linkages is essential for unlocking this potential and creating opportunities for smallholder farmers and agribusinesses."

To provide a tangible example, Mr. Mensah arranged for Alex to visit a food processing facility in Ghana, where farmers' produce was transformed into value-added products for domestic and export markets. They toured the facility, witnessing the sophisticated machinery and skilled workers as they processed and packaged a variety of agricultural products.

"As a food processor, our goal is to add value to agricultural products, create new markets, and generate income for farmers," one manager explained. "Through investment in technology and training, we can improve our production processes, increase our productivity, and compete in local and international markets."

As they delved deeper into the discussion, Mr. Mensah emphasized the importance of collaboration and innovation in developing agribusiness value chains. "Agribusiness value chains require close coordination and collaboration among farmers, processors, traders, and other stakeholders," he said. "By working together and leveraging each other's strengths, we can create value, drive growth, and improve livelihoods across the agricultural sector."

Later that afternoon, Mr. Mensah arranged for Alex to attend a workshop on agribusiness value chain development in Africa. The event brought together stakeholders from across the agricultural sector to discuss strategies for strengthening value chains, improving market access, and promoting inclusive growth.

Alex found the workshop enlightening, gaining valuable insights into the challenges and opportunities facing agribusiness value chains in Africa. He was impressed by the innovative approaches and collaborative spirit of the participants in addressing the complexities of value chain development and unlocking the potential of Africa's agricultural sector.

As the day came to a close, Alex thanked Mr. Mensah for his insights and hospitality. He left his office feeling more determined than ever to explore opportunities for investment in agribusiness value chains in Africa.

Back at his hotel, Alex reflected on the day's discussions. Agribusiness value chains were not just about adding value to agricultural products; they were about creating opportunities, improving livelihoods, and driving economic development. Armed with this understanding, he felt ready to pursue investment opportunities that would not only generate returns but also contribute to the growth and prosperity of Africa's agricultural sector.

7.3: Investment in Agricultural Technology

As the sun reached its zenith, Alex delved deeper into agricultural investment opportunities, focusing on the transformative potential of agricultural technology. His next meeting awaited him with Dr. Amina Nwosu, a leading researcher in agricultural innovation and technology.

Dr. Nwosu welcomed Alex into her office, which was adorned with posters showcasing the latest advancements in agricultural technology. "Good afternoon, Alex," she greeted warmly. "Today, we'll explore the exciting world of agricultural technology and the opportunities it presents for improving productivity, efficiency, and sustainability in Africa's agriculture sector."

Eager to learn, Alex settled into his seat as Dr. Nwosu began to elucidate the significance of agricultural technology. "Agricultural technology, or agritech, encompasses a wide range of innovations and solutions aimed at improving various aspects of agricultural production, from crop cultivation and livestock management to pest control and irrigation," she explained. "From precision farming and drone technology to biotechnology and digital agriculture, agritech is revolutionizing the way we farm and helping to address some of the key challenges facing agriculture in Africa."

She highlighted the challenges facing agriculture in Africa, including limited access to modern farming techniques, climate change, and shrinking arable land. "Agricultural technology offers a solution to these challenges by providing farmers with access to innovative tools and techniques to improve their yields, reduce their environmental impact, and increase their resilience to climate change," Dr. Nwosu said. "Investment in agricultural technology is essential for unlocking this potential and driving sustainable agricultural development across the continent."

To provide a tangible example, Dr. Nwosu arranged for Alex to visit a research institute in Nigeria, where scientists were developing drought-resistant crop varieties using advanced biotechnology. They toured the laboratories, witnessing the groundbreaking research and innovation taking place.

"As a scientist, our goal is to develop crop varieties that can withstand the challenges of climate change and provide farmers with reliable and resilient options for improving their yields," one researcher explained. "Through investment in research and development, we can unlock the full potential of agricultural technology to address some of the most pressing challenges facing agriculture in Africa."

As they delved deeper into the discussion, Dr. Nwosu emphasized the importance of collaboration and partnerships in driving agricultural technology innovation. "Agricultural technology development requires close collaboration between researchers, farmers, policymakers, and the private sector," she said. "By working together and leveraging each other's expertise and resources, we can accelerate the adoption of agricultural technology and drive sustainable agricultural development across Africa."

Later that afternoon, Dr. Nwosu arranged for Alex to attend

a symposium on agricultural technology innovation in Africa. The event brought together researchers, entrepreneurs, and policymakers to discuss strategies for promoting technology adoption and innovation in the agriculture sector.

Alex found the symposium enlightening, gaining valuable insights into the transformative potential of agricultural technology in Africa. He was inspired by the passion and dedication of the participants in harnessing technology to address the challenges facing agriculture and improve livelihoods across the continent.

As the day came to a close, Alex thanked Dr. Nwosu for her insights and hospitality. He left her office feeling more determined than ever to explore opportunities for investment in agricultural technology in Africa.

Back at his hotel, Alex reflected on the day's discussions. Agricultural technology was not just about innovation; it was about empowering farmers, improving livelihoods, and driving sustainable development across Africa. Armed with this understanding, he felt ready to pursue investment opportunities that would not only generate returns but also contribute to the advancement of Africa's agriculture sector.

7.4: Land Ownership and Regulatory Issues

As the afternoon sun cast long shadows over the landscape, Alex delved into the complexities of agricultural investment, turning his attention to the crucial issues of land ownership and regulatory frameworks. His next meeting awaited him with Ms. Fatou Diallo, a legal expert specializing in land tenure and agricultural regulation.

Ms. Diallo welcomed Alex into her office, which was

adorned with legal texts and maps depicting land tenure systems across Africa. "Good afternoon, Alex," she greeted warmly. "Today, we'll explore the critical issues of land ownership and regulatory frameworks in agricultural investment in Africa."

Eager to learn, Alex settled into his seat as Ms. Diallo began to elucidate the significance of land ownership. "Land ownership is a fundamental aspect of agricultural investment, providing farmers and investors with the security and stability they need to make long-term investments in agricultural production," she explained. "However, land tenure systems in Africa are often complex and fragmented, with multiple competing claims to land and overlapping rights."

She highlighted the challenges facing land ownership in Africa, including insecure land tenure, land grabbing, and conflicts over land rights. "These challenges can create uncertainty and risk for investors, discouraging investment in agricultural production and limiting opportunities for smallholder farmers to access land and resources," Ms. Diallo said. "Addressing these challenges requires clear and transparent land tenure systems, effective land governance mechanisms, and policies that protect the rights of all stakeholders."

To provide a tangible example, Ms. Diallo arranged for Alex to visit a rural community in Senegal, where farmers were struggling to secure land rights amidst competing claims and encroachment from large-scale agribusinesses. They met with community leaders and farmers, who shared their stories of land tenure insecurity and the impact it was having on their livelihoods.

"As smallholder farmers, land is our most valuable asset," one farmer explained. "But without secure land rights, we cannot invest in our farms or plan for the future. We need clear and transparent land tenure systems that protect our rights and ensure that we can access the land we need to feed our families and communities."

As they delved deeper into the discussion, Ms. Diallo emphasized the importance of regulatory frameworks in supporting agricultural investment and protecting the rights of all stakeholders. "Regulatory frameworks play a crucial role in providing the legal and institutional framework necessary for agricultural investment to flourish," she said. "From land tenure laws and property rights to environmental regulations and investment incentives, effective regulatory frameworks can provide the certainty and stability investors need to make long-term commitments to agricultural production."

Later that afternoon, Ms. Diallo arranged for Alex to attend a workshop on land tenure and agricultural regulation in Africa. The event brought together policymakers, legal experts, and civil society organizations to discuss strategies for improving land governance and regulatory frameworks to support agricultural investment and rural development.

Alex found the workshop enlightening, gaining valuable insights into the challenges and opportunities facing land ownership and regulatory issues in agricultural investment in Africa. He was inspired by the dedication and commitment of the participants in finding innovative solutions to these complex challenges and creating an enabling environment for agricultural investment to thrive.

As the day came to a close, Alex thanked Ms. Diallo for her insights and hospitality. He left her office feeling more determined than ever to explore opportunities for investment in agriculture in Africa, knowing that addressing land ownership and regulatory issues would be crucial to unlocking the full potential of the continent's agricultural sector.

Back at his hotel, Alex reflected on the day's discussions. Land ownership and regulatory issues were not just legal matters; they were fundamental to the success of agricultural investment and rural development in Africa. Armed with this understanding, he felt ready to pursue investment opportunities that would not only generate returns but also contribute to building a more inclusive and sustainable agricultural sector across the continent.

7.5: Sustainable Agricultural Practices

As the sun dipped below the horizon, casting a warm glow over the landscape, Alex delved deeper into agricultural investment opportunities, focusing on the imperative of sustainable agricultural practices. His next meeting awaited him with Dr. Ibrahim Kamara, a renowned agronomist and advocate for sustainable farming techniques.

Dr. Kamara welcomed Alex into his office, which was adorned with charts and diagrams illustrating the principles of sustainable agriculture. "Good evening, Alex," he greeted warmly. "Today, we'll explore the importance of sustainable agricultural practices and the opportunities they present for improving productivity, resilience, and environmental sustainability in Africa's agriculture sector."

Eager to learn, Alex settled into his seat as Dr. Kamara began to elucidate the significance of sustainable agriculture. "Sustainable agriculture is about meeting the needs of the present without compromising the ability of future generations to meet their own needs," he explained. "It involves adopting farming techniques and practices that are environmentally friendly, socially responsible, and economically viable."

He highlighted the challenges facing agriculture in Africa, including soil degradation, water scarcity, and loss of biodiversity. "These challenges are exacerbated by climate change and unsustainable farming practices, which degrade natural resources and undermine the long-term viability of agricultural production systems," Dr. Kamara said. "Investment in sustainable agriculture is essential for addressing these challenges and building resilient and inclusive food systems that can sustainably feed Africa's growing population."

To provide a tangible example, Dr. Kamara arranged for Alex to visit a sustainable farm in Kenya, where farmers were practicing agroecology and regenerative agriculture techniques. They toured the farm, witnessing the diverse crops and livestock, as well as the innovative farming methods being employed.

"As farmers, our goal is to produce food in a way that nourishes the land, conserves natural resources, and enhances biodiversity," one farmer explained. "Through investment in sustainable farming practices, we can improve our soil health, increase our yields, and reduce our environmental impact, while also improving the livelihoods of our communities."

As they delved deeper into the discussion, Dr. Kamara emphasized the importance of knowledge sharing and capacity building in promoting sustainable agriculture. "Sustainable agriculture requires a shift in mindset and behavior, as well as access to training, information, and resources," he said. "By investing in farmer education and extension services, we can empower farmers to adopt sustainable farming practices and drive positive change in their communities."

Later that evening, Dr. Kamara arranged for Alex to attend a seminar on sustainable agriculture innovation in Africa. The event brought together researchers, policymakers, and farmers to discuss strategies for promoting sustainable farming practices and scaling up successful initiatives across the continent.

Alex found the seminar enlightening, gaining valuable insights into the transformative potential of sustainable agriculture in Africa. He was inspired by the passion and commitment of the participants in harnessing sustainable farming techniques to address the challenges facing agriculture and improve livelihoods across the continent.

As the night came to a close, Alex thanked Dr. Kamara for his insights and hospitality. He left his office feeling more determined than ever to explore opportunities for investment in sustainable agriculture in Africa.

Back at his hotel, Alex reflected on the day's discussions. Sustainable agriculture was not just about producing food; it was about nurturing the land, protecting the environment, and ensuring the well-being of future generations. Armed with this understanding, he felt ready to pursue investment opportunities that would not only generate returns but also contribute to building a more sustainable and resilient agriculture sector across Africa.

7.6: Summary and Conclusion

As the stars twinkled in the night sky, Alex concluded his exploration of agricultural investment opportunities, reflecting on the wealth of insights gained throughout the day. His final meeting was with Dr. Maryam Mbeki, a seasoned economist and advocate for agricultural development in Africa.

Dr. Mbeki welcomed Alex into her office, a sanctuary of knowledge adorned with maps and charts depicting the agricultural landscape of Africa. "Good evening, Alex," she greeted warmly. "Today, we've embarked on a journey through the world of agricultural investment opportunities in Africa, exploring the importance of agriculture, agribusiness value chains, agricultural technology, land ownership, sustainable practices, and more."

Eager to summarize their discussions, Dr. Mbeki began to elucidate the key takeaways from their exploration. "Throughout our journey, we've seen how agriculture is not just a sector; it's a way of life for millions of people across Africa," she said. "From smallholder farmers and agribusinesses to investors and policymakers, agriculture is central to Africa's economy, society, and future."

She highlighted the challenges facing agriculture in Africa, including land tenure insecurity, climate change, and unsustainable farming practices. "Despite these challenges, Africa has immense agricultural potential, with vast arable land, abundant water resources, and a rich diversity of crops and livestock," Dr. Mbeki said. "Investment in agriculture is essential for unlocking this potential, improving productivity, and ensuring the sustainability of food production systems."

To provide a final reflection, Dr. Mbeki emphasized the importance of collaboration, innovation, and sustainability in driving agricultural investment and development in Africa. "By working together and leveraging each other's strengths, we can create opportunities, improve livelihoods, and build a more resilient and inclusive agriculture sector across the continent," she said.

As their meeting came to a close, Dr. Mbeki thanked Alex for his engagement and curiosity throughout their discussions. "I hope our journey has provided you with valuable insights into the exciting opportunities and challenges of agricultural investment in Africa," she said. "By investing in agriculture, you have the opportunity to not only generate financial returns but also make a meaningful impact on the lives of millions of people across the continent."

Alex left Dr. Mbeki's office feeling inspired and enlightened by their conversation. Agriculture was not just about farming; it was about feeding communities, creating livelihoods, and driving economic development. Armed with a deeper understanding of the importance of agriculture in Africa's development, Alex felt ready to embark on his journey as an investor, knowing that his contributions would help shape Africa's agricultural future.

As he stepped out into the cool night air, Alex gazed up at the stars, filled with hope and excitement for the possibilities that lay ahead. Africa's agricultural landscape was vast and diverse, and he was ready to be a part of it, making a difference one investment at a time.

8

Chapter 8: Energy and Natural Resources

8.1: Overview of Africa's Energy Landscape

As the sun rose over the horizon, Alex embarked on a new chapter of exploration, delving into Africa's energy and natural resources sector. His journey began with a meeting with Dr. Fatima Ibrahim, a leading expert in energy economics and sustainable development.

Dr. Ibrahim welcomed Alex into her office, which was adorned with maps and diagrams depicting Africa's energy landscape. "Good morning, Alex," she greeted warmly. "Today, we'll delve into the intricate world of energy and natural resources in Africa, exploring the opportunities and challenges that lie ahead."

Eager to learn, Alex settled into his seat as Dr. Ibrahim began to elucidate the significance of Africa's energy landscape. "Africa is endowed with abundant energy resources, including oil, gas, coal, hydroelectric, solar, and wind power," she explained. "However, despite this wealth of resources, many countries in Africa still face significant energy challenges, including energy poverty, limited access to electricity, and reliance on fossil fuels."

She highlighted the diversity of Africa's energy mix, with different countries harnessing different energy sources based on their geographical, economic, and environmental conditions. "From oil-rich countries in North Africa to hydroelectric powerhouses in East Africa and solar energy pioneers in the Sahel region, Africa's energy landscape is as diverse as its people and cultures," Dr. Ibrahim said.

To provide a tangible example, Dr. Ibrahim arranged for Alex to visit a solar power plant in Rwanda, where the sun's rays were being harnessed to generate clean and renewable electricity for the local community. They toured the facility, witnessing the gleaming solar panels and sophisticated technology that powered the plant.

"As a renewable energy developer, our goal is to harness the power of the sun to provide clean and sustainable electricity to communities across Africa," one engineer explained. "Through investment in solar energy, we can reduce our dependence on fossil fuels, mitigate climate change, and improve energy access for millions of people."

As they delved deeper into the discussion, Dr. Ibrahim emphasized the importance of sustainable energy development in Africa's future. "Sustainable energy development is essential for addressing the dual challenges of energy poverty and climate change," she said. "By investing in renewable energy sources, improving energy efficiency, and adopting clean technologies, Africa can unlock its energy potential while also contributing to global efforts to combat climate change."

Later that morning, Dr. Ibrahim arranged for Alex to attend a conference on energy and natural resources in Africa. The event brought together policymakers, industry leaders, and civil society organizations to discuss strategies for promoting sustainable energy development and natural resource management across the continent.

Alex found the conference enlightening, gaining valuable insights into the opportunities and challenges facing Africa's energy and natural resources sector. He was inspired by the passion and commitment of the participants in finding innovative solutions to address energy poverty, improve energy access, and promote sustainable development across the continent.

As the day came to a close, Alex thanked Dr. Ibrahim for her insights and hospitality. He left her office feeling more determined than ever to explore opportunities for investment in energy and natural resources in Africa.

Back at his hotel, Alex reflected on the day's discussions. Africa's energy landscape was vast and diverse, with opportunities for investment in renewable energy, oil and gas, mining, and more. Armed with this understanding, he felt ready to pursue investment opportunities that would not only generate returns but also contribute to the sustainable development of Africa's energy and natural resources sector.

8.2: Renewable Energy Opportunities

As the midday sun beat down on the landscape, Alex delved deeper into Africa's energy sector, focusing his attention on the promising opportunities within renewable energy. His next meeting awaited him with Mr. Jamal Mubarak, a leading entrepreneur in the renewable energy sector.

Mr. Mubarak welcomed Alex into his office, which was adorned with posters showcasing wind turbines, solar panels, and hydroelectric dams. "Good afternoon, Alex," he greeted warmly. "Today, we'll explore the exciting world of renewable energy opportunities in Africa and the transformative impact they can have on the continent's energy landscape."

Eager to learn, Alex settled into his seat as Mr. Mubarak began to elucidate the significance of renewable energy. "Renewable energy sources, such as solar, wind, hydro, and geothermal power, offer clean, sustainable alternatives to traditional fossil fuels," he explained. "In Africa, where energy demand is growing rapidly, renewable energy presents a unique opportunity to meet this demand while also addressing energy poverty, reducing greenhouse gas emissions, and promoting sustainable development."

He highlighted the abundance of renewable energy resources in Africa, from the sun-soaked deserts of the Sahara to the wind-swept plains of the Horn of Africa and the mighty rivers of the Congo Basin. "Africa has some of the best renewable energy resources in the world, with vast untapped potential for solar, wind, hydro, and geothermal power," Mr. Mubarak said.

To provide a tangible example, Mr. Mubarak arranged for Alex to visit a solar farm in South Africa, where rows of solar panels stretched as far as the eye could see, harnessing the power of the sun to generate electricity for homes and businesses. They toured the facility, witnessing the gleaming panels and innovative technology that powered the farm.

"As a renewable energy developer, our goal is to harness the abundant solar energy in Africa to provide clean, reliable electricity to communities across the continent," one engineer explained. "Through investment in solar energy, we can reduce our dependence on fossil fuels, create jobs, and improve energy access for millions of people."

As they delved deeper into the discussion, Mr. Mubarak emphasized the importance of policy support and investment incentives in driving renewable energy development in Africa. "Government policies and incentives play a crucial role in creating an enabling environment for renewable energy investment," he said. "By providing support for renewable energy projects, such as feed-in tariffs, tax incentives, and regulatory frameworks, governments can attract investment, stimulate innovation, and accelerate the transition to a sustainable energy future."

Later that afternoon, Mr. Mubarak arranged for Alex to attend a summit on renewable energy investment in Africa. The event brought together investors, policymakers, and industry leaders to discuss strategies for promoting renewable energy development and unlocking the continent's clean energy potential.

Alex found the summit enlightening, gaining valuable insights into the opportunities and challenges facing renewable energy investment in Africa. He was inspired by the passion and commitment of the participants in harnessing renewable energy to address energy poverty, mitigate climate change, and drive sustainable development across the continent.

As the day came to a close, Alex thanked Mr. Mubarak for his insights and hospitality. He left his office feeling more determined than ever to explore opportunities for investment in renewable energy in Africa.

Back at his hotel, Alex reflected on the day's discussions.

Renewable energy was not just a solution to Africa's energy challenges; it was a catalyst for economic growth, environmental sustainability, and social progress. Armed with this understanding, he felt ready to pursue investment opportunities that would not only generate returns but also contribute to the transition to a clean energy future in Africa.

8.3: Oil and Gas Sector

As the afternoon sun cast a warm glow over the cityscape, Alex delved into another facet of Africa's energy landscape, turning his attention to the pivotal role of the oil and gas sector. His next meeting awaited him with Mr. Malik Abadi, a seasoned executive in the oil and gas industry.

Mr. Abadi welcomed Alex into his office, a testament to the industry's prestige with maps displaying oil fields and rigs. "Good afternoon, Alex," he greeted warmly. "Today, we'll explore the dynamic world of Africa's oil and gas sector and the opportunities it presents for investment and growth."

Eager to learn, Alex settled into his seat as Mr. Abadi began to elucidate the significance of the oil and gas sector. "Africa is home to abundant reserves of oil and natural gas, making it a key player in the global energy market," he explained. "From the oil-rich fields of Nigeria and Angola to the emerging gas hubs of Mozambique and Tanzania, Africa's oil and gas sector offers significant investment opportunities across the value chain."

He highlighted the importance of the oil and gas sector to Africa's economy, providing vital revenue streams, employment opportunities, and infrastructure development. "The oil and gas sector is a cornerstone of Africa's economy, driving economic growth, industrialization, and social development," Mr. Abadi said.

To provide a tangible example, Mr. Abadi arranged for Alex to visit an offshore oil rig in Ghana, where drilling operations were underway to extract crude oil from deep beneath the ocean floor. They toured the rig, witnessing the sophisticated machinery and skilled workers as they extracted oil from the seabed.

"As an oil and gas producer, our goal is to harness Africa's natural resources to meet the world's energy needs while also benefiting the local economy and community," one engineer explained. "Through investment in technology and expertise, we can maximize the potential of Africa's oil and gas reserves and ensure that they contribute to sustainable development and prosperity."

As they delved deeper into the discussion, Mr. Abadi emphasized the importance of responsible and sustainable practices in the oil and gas sector. "Responsible resource management and environmental stewardship are essential for ensuring the long-term viability of Africa's oil and gas sector," he said. "By adhering to high environmental and social standards, we can minimize the impact of our operations on the environment and local communities and ensure that the benefits of resource extraction are shared equitably."

Later that afternoon, Mr. Abadi arranged for Alex to attend a conference on oil and gas investment in Africa. The event brought together industry leaders, policymakers, and investors to discuss strategies for promoting sustainable development and responsible investment in the oil and gas sector.

Alex found the conference enlightening, gaining valuable insights into the opportunities and challenges facing the oil and gas sector in Africa. He was impressed by the industry's commitment to responsible resource management and sustainable development, as well as its potential to drive economic growth and development across the continent.

As the day came to a close, Alex thanked Mr. Abadi for his insights and hospitality. He left his office feeling more determined than ever to explore opportunities for investment in the oil and gas sector in Africa.

Back at his hotel, Alex reflected on the day's discussions. The oil and gas sector was not without its challenges, but with the right approach and investment, it had the potential to contribute significantly to Africa's energy security and economic development. Armed with this understanding, he felt ready to pursue investment opportunities that would not only generate returns but also contribute to the sustainable development of Africa's oil and gas sector.

8.4: Mining and Minerals

As the sun dipped below the horizon, casting a golden hue over the landscape, Alex ventured further into Africa's energy and natural resources sector, focusing his attention on the vast opportunities within mining and minerals. His next meeting awaited him with Ms. Aisha Mansour, a seasoned geologist with expertise in mineral exploration and mining operations.

Ms. Mansour welcomed Alex into her office, a space adorned with geological maps and mineral samples from across the continent. "Good evening, Alex," she greeted warmly. "Today, we'll explore the rich tapestry of Africa's mining and minerals sector and the wealth of opportunities it holds for investment and development."

Eager to learn, Alex settled into his seat as Ms. Mansour began to elucidate the significance of mining and minerals. "Africa is blessed with abundant mineral resources, including gold, diamonds, copper, cobalt, and platinum, among others," she explained. "From the gold mines of South Africa to the diamond fields of Botswana and the copper belts of Zambia and the Democratic Republic of Congo, Africa's mining sector offers a diverse array of investment opportunities."

She highlighted the importance of the mining and minerals sector to Africa's economy, providing vital revenue streams, employment opportunities, and infrastructure development. "The mining and minerals sector is a cornerstone of Africa's economy, driving economic growth, industrialization, and social development," Ms. Mansour said.

To provide a tangible example, Ms. Mansour arranged for Alex to visit a diamond mine in Botswana, where miners were hard at work extracting rough diamonds from deep underground. They toured the mine, witnessing the intricate process of diamond extraction and processing.

"As a miner, our goal is to extract minerals in a responsible and sustainable manner, ensuring that the benefits of mining are shared equitably among all stakeholders," one miner explained. "Through investment in technology, safety, and community development, we can maximize the positive impact of mining on the local economy and environment."

As they delved deeper into the discussion, Ms. Mansour emphasized the importance of responsible and sustainable practices in the mining and minerals sector. "Responsible mining practices are essential for minimizing the environmental impact of mining operations and ensuring that the benefits of resource extraction are shared equitably among all stakeholders," she said. "By adhering to high environmental and social standards, we can mitigate the negative impacts of mining on local communities and ecosystems and ensure that mining contributes to sustainable development and prosperity."

Later that evening, Ms. Mansour arranged for Alex to attend a conference on mining and minerals investment in Africa. The event brought together industry leaders, policymakers, and investors to discuss strategies for promoting responsible mining practices and sustainable development in the mining sector.

Alex found the conference enlightening, gaining valuable insights into the opportunities and challenges facing the mining and minerals sector in Africa. He was impressed by the industry's commitment to responsible resource management and sustainable development, as well as its potential to drive economic growth and development across the continent.

As the night came to a close, Alex thanked Ms. Mansour for her insights and hospitality. He left her office feeling more determined than ever to explore opportunities for investment in the mining and minerals sector in Africa.

Back at his hotel, Alex reflected on the day's discussions. The mining and minerals sector was a pillar of Africa's economy, offering vast opportunities for investment and development. Armed with this understanding, he felt ready to pursue investment opportunities that would not only generate returns but also contribute to the sustainable development of Africa's mining and minerals sector.

8.5: Environmental Considerations

As the dawn broke, painting the sky with hues of orange and pink, Alex delved deeper into Africa's energy and natural resources sector, turning his attention to the critical aspect of environmental considerations. His next meeting awaited him with Dr. Fatima Mbeki, an environmental scientist and advocate for sustainable resource management.

Dr. Mbeki welcomed Alex into her office, a serene space adorned with images of pristine landscapes and endangered species. "Good morning, Alex," she greeted warmly. "Today, we'll explore the vital role of environmental considerations in Africa's energy and natural resources sector and the importance of sustainable resource management for the future of our planet."

Eager to learn, Alex settled into his seat as Dr. Mbeki began to elucidate the significance of environmental considerations. "Africa's energy and natural resources sector plays a crucial role in driving economic growth and development, but it also poses significant environmental challenges," she explained. "From deforestation and habitat destruction to air and water pollution, the extraction and use of energy and natural resources can have profound impacts on the environment and biodiversity."

She highlighted the importance of integrating environmental considerations into decision-making processes across the energy and natural resources sector. "Environmental considerations are not just about protecting the environment; they're also about safeguarding human health, preserving biodiversity, and ensuring the long-term sustainability of our natural resources," Dr. Mbeki said.

To provide a tangible example, Dr. Mbeki arranged for Alex to visit a mining site in Ghana, where miners were extracting gold from deep underground. They toured the site, witnessing the intricate process of gold extraction and processing, as well as the environmental management measures in place to minimize the impact of mining on the surrounding ecosystem.

"As a mining company, our goal is to operate in a way that minimizes our environmental footprint and maximizes our positive contribution to local communities and ecosystems," one environmental manager explained. "Through investment in environmental management practices, reclamation efforts, and community engagement, we can ensure that our mining activities are conducted in a responsible and sustainable manner."

As they delved deeper into the discussion, Dr. Mbeki emphasized the importance of stakeholder engagement and collaboration in addressing environmental challenges in the energy and natural resources sector. "Environmental protection is a collective responsibility that requires the participation of governments, industry, civil society, and local communities," she said. "By working together and sharing knowledge, resources, and best practices, we can find innovative solutions to environmental challenges and create a more sustainable future for all."

Later that morning, Dr. Mbeki arranged for Alex to attend a seminar on environmental management in the energy and natural resources sector. The event brought together experts, policymakers, and stakeholders to discuss strategies for promoting environmental stewardship and sustainability in resource extraction and energy production.

Alex found the seminar enlightening, gaining valuable

insights into the importance of environmental considerations in the energy and natural resources sector. He was impressed by the commitment of the participants to finding solutions to environmental challenges and ensuring that resource extraction and energy production are conducted in a responsible and sustainable manner.

As the day came to a close, Alex thanked Dr. Mbeki for her insights and hospitality. He left her office feeling more determined than ever to explore opportunities for investment in the energy and natural resources sector in Africa, knowing that environmental considerations would be at the forefront of his decision-making process.

Back at his hotel, Alex reflected on the day's discussions. Environmental considerations were not just about compliance; they were about ethics, responsibility, and ensuring a sustainable future for generations to come. Armed with this understanding, he felt ready to pursue investment opportunities that would not only generate returns but also contribute to the protection and preservation of Africa's natural environment.

8.6: Summary and Conclusion

As the sun began to set on another day of exploration, Alex prepared to wrap up his journey through Africa's energy and natural resources sector. His final meeting awaited him with Dr. Samuel Okonjo, a renowned economist and advocate for sustainable development.

Dr. Okonjo welcomed Alex into his office, a space adorned with maps and charts depicting Africa's energy and natural resources landscape. "Good evening, Alex," he greeted warmly. "Today, we've embarked on a journey through the dynamic world of Africa's energy and natural resources sector, exploring the diverse opportunities and challenges it presents for investment and development."

Eager to summarize their discussions, Dr. Okonjo began to elucidate the key takeaways from their exploration. "Throughout our journey, we've seen how Africa's energy and natural resources sector is a cornerstone of the continent's economy, driving economic growth, industrialization, and social development," he said. "From renewable energy to oil and gas, mining, and environmental considerations, the sector offers a wealth of opportunities for investment and growth."

He highlighted the importance of responsible and sustainable practices in the energy and natural resources sector, emphasizing the need to balance economic development with environmental protection and social responsibility. "Sustainable resource management is essential for ensuring the long-term viability of Africa's energy and natural resources sector and safeguarding the well-being of future generations," Dr. Okonjo said.

To provide a final reflection, Dr. Okonjo emphasized the importance of collaboration, innovation, and inclusivity in driving sustainable development in the energy and natural resources sector. "By working together and leveraging each other's strengths, we can overcome the challenges facing the sector and unlock its full potential to drive economic growth, promote social progress, and protect the environment," he said.

As their meeting came to a close, Dr. Okonjo thanked Alex for his engagement and curiosity throughout their discussions. "I hope our journey has provided you with valuable insights into the exciting opportunities and challenges of investing in Africa's energy and natural resources sector," he said. "By investing in sustainable development, you have the opportunity to not only generate financial returns but also make a meaningful impact on the lives of millions of people across the continent."

Alex left Dr. Okonjo's office feeling inspired and enlightened by their conversation. Africa's energy and natural resources sector was vast and diverse, offering opportunities for investment and growth that could drive sustainable development and prosperity across the continent. Armed with this understanding, he felt ready to embark on his journey as an investor, knowing that his contributions would help shape Africa's energy and natural resources future.

As he stepped out into the cool night air, Alex gazed up at the stars, filled with hope and excitement for the possibilities that lay ahead. Africa's energy and natural resources sector held the key to unlocking a brighter future for generations to come, and he was eager to be a part of it, making a difference one investment at a time.

Chapter 9: Real Estate and Urban Development

9.1: Urbanization Trends in Africa

As the sun rose over the vibrant cityscape, Alex delved into the intricate world of real estate and urban development in Africa, recognizing it as a pivotal aspect of the continent's economic growth and transformation. His journey began with a meeting with Dr. Fatima Sow, an urban planner renowned for her expertise in analyzing urbanization trends across Africa.

Dr. Sow welcomed Alex into her office, a space adorned with maps, charts, and graphs depicting the dynamic evolution of cities across the continent. "Good morning, Alex," she greeted warmly. "Today, we'll explore the urbanization trends shaping Africa's real estate and urban development landscape."

Eager to learn, Alex settled into his seat as Dr. Sow began to elucidate the intricacies of urbanization trends in Africa. "Urbanization is one of the most significant demographic trends occurring on the continent," she explained. "As populations grow and economies expand, cities are experiencing rapid growth and transformation, presenting both opportunities and challenges for real estate and urban development."

She highlighted the key drivers and characteristics of urbanization in Africa, emphasizing the importance of understanding the unique dynamics and complexities of urban growth in diverse contexts. "Urbanization in Africa is characterized by a myriad of factors, including population growth, rural-to-urban migration, and economic development," Dr. Sow said. "Each city presents its own set of opportunities and challenges, requiring tailored approaches and strategies for sustainable urban development."

To provide a tangible example, Dr. Sow arranged for Alex to visit a rapidly growing city on the continent. They toured bustling streets, vibrant markets, and burgeoning residential neighborhoods, witnessing firsthand the dynamic transformation underway.

"As populations continue to flock to urban centers in search of better opportunities, cities are grappling with a host of challenges, including housing shortages, inadequate infrastructure, and environmental degradation," Dr. Sow explained. "However, with proper planning and investment, these challenges can be transformed into opportunities for sustainable growth and development."

As they delved deeper into the discussion, Dr. Sow emphasized the importance of adopting holistic approaches to urban development that prioritize inclusivity, resilience, and sustainability. "Urbanization in Africa presents a unique opportunity to reimagine cities as vibrant, inclusive, and sustainable hubs of economic activity and innovation," she said. "By prioritizing investments in affordable housing, public transportation, and green infrastructure, cities can become more livable, resilient, and prosperous for all residents."

Later that day, Dr. Sow arranged for Alex to attend a conference on urbanization trends in Africa. The conference brought together policymakers, urban planners, and real estate developers to discuss best practices and strategies for addressing the complex challenges and opportunities of urban growth on the continent.

Alex found the conference enlightening, gaining valuable insights into the multifaceted nature of urbanization in Africa and the diverse approaches to urban development being implemented across the continent. He was impressed by the emphasis placed on sustainability, inclusivity, and innovation in driving urban transformation, as well as the importance of collaboration and partnership in addressing the complex challenges of urban growth.

As the day came to a close, Alex thanked Dr. Sow for her insights and hospitality. He left her office feeling more informed and inspired than ever to explore opportunities for real estate and urban development in Africa, knowing that urbanization would be key to unlocking opportunities and driving growth in the dynamic and evolving cities of the continent.

Back at his hotel, Alex reflected on the day's discussions. Urbanization in Africa was not just a demographic trend; it was a transformative force reshaping the continent's cities and economies. Armed with this understanding, he felt ready to embark on his journey of exploring real estate and urban development opportunities in Africa, knowing that the strategies and insights he gained would be instrumental in driving sustainable growth and prosperity for all stakeholders involved.

9.2: Residential and Commercial Real Estate

As the day progressed, Alex delved deeper into the world of real estate and urban development, focusing now on the dynamics of residential and commercial properties across Africa. His next meeting awaited him with Mr. Ibrahim Kamara, a seasoned real estate developer renowned for his expertise in navigating the diverse markets of the continent.

Mr. Kamara welcomed Alex into his office, a space adorned with blueprints, architectural models, and photos showcasing the diverse portfolio of residential and commercial properties he had developed across Africa. "Good afternoon, Alex," he greeted warmly. "Today, we'll explore the complexities of residential and commercial real estate in Africa and the opportunities they present for investors and developers."

Eager to learn, Alex settled into his seat as Mr. Kamara began to elucidate the intricacies of real estate development in Africa. "Real estate in Africa is a dynamic and rapidly evolving sector, driven by urbanization, population growth, and economic expansion," he explained. "Residential and commercial properties play a central role in meeting the diverse housing and business needs of growing urban populations."

He highlighted the key trends and characteristics of residential and commercial real estate in Africa, emphasizing the importance of understanding local market dynamics, regulatory frameworks, and consumer preferences. "Residential real estate encompasses a wide range of housing options, from affordable housing for low-income families to luxury apartments and gated communities for high-net-worth individuals," Mr. Kamara said. "Commercial real estate, on the other hand, includes office buildings, retail centers, industrial parks, and hospitality properties that support economic activity and business growth."

To provide a tangible example, Mr. Kamara arranged for Alex to tour a mixed-use development project underway in a rapidly growing city. They explored residential apartments, office spaces, retail outlets, and recreational facilities, witnessing firsthand the integration of different property types to create vibrant and sustainable urban environments.

"As urban populations continue to grow and economies expand, demand for both residential and commercial real estate is on the rise," Mr. Kamara explained. "Investors and developers have a unique opportunity to capitalize on this demand by delivering high-quality, innovative, and sustainable real estate solutions that meet the diverse needs of urban residents and businesses."

As they delved deeper into the discussion, Mr. Kamara emphasized the importance of adopting a holistic approach to real estate development that prioritizes sustainability, inclusivity, and community engagement. "Real estate development is not just about building structures; it's about creating vibrant, livable, and resilient communities that enhance quality of life and promote economic prosperity," he said. "By integrating sustainable design principles, green technologies, and community amenities into their projects, developers can create lasting value for both investors and society."

Later that afternoon, Mr. Kamara arranged for Alex to attend a real estate conference focusing on residential and commercial properties in Africa. The conference brought together investors, developers, policymakers, and industry experts to discuss market trends, investment opportunities, and best practices for real estate development across the continent.

Alex found the conference enlightening, gaining valuable insights into the diverse opportunities and challenges of residential and commercial real estate in Africa. He was impressed by the innovative approaches and sustainable solutions being implemented by developers to address the housing and business needs of urban populations, as well as the importance of collaboration and partnership in driving successful real estate projects.

As the day came to a close, Alex thanked Mr. Kamara for his insights and hospitality. He left his office feeling more informed and inspired than ever to explore opportunities for real estate development in Africa, knowing that residential and commercial properties would play a crucial role in shaping the future of the continent's cities and economies.

Back at his hotel, Alex reflected on the day's discussions. Residential and commercial real estate in Africa was not just about bricks and mortar; it was about creating vibrant, inclusive, and sustainable urban environments that enhance quality of life and promote economic growth. Armed with this understanding, he felt ready to embark on his journey of exploring real estate opportunities in Africa, knowing that the projects he invested in would have a lasting impact on the communities they served.

9.3: Affordable Housing Initiatives

As the day unfolded, Alex delved into the critical issue of affordable housing initiatives in Africa, recognizing the pressing need to address housing challenges for the continent's growing urban populations. His next meeting awaited him with Ms. Aisha Nkrumah, a passionate advocate for affordable housing and community development.

Ms. Nkrumah welcomed Alex into her office, a space adorned with posters depicting thriving communities and successful housing projects. "Good afternoon, Alex," she greeted warmly. "Today, we'll explore the importance of affordable housing initiatives in Africa and the transformative impact they can have on people's lives."

Eager to learn, Alex settled into his seat as Ms. Nkrumah began to elucidate the intricacies of affordable housing initiatives. "Access to affordable housing is a fundamental human right and a cornerstone of sustainable development," she explained. "Yet, millions of people across Africa lack access to safe, decent, and affordable housing, forcing them to live in informal settlements or slums with inadequate infrastructure and services."

She highlighted the key challenges and barriers to affordable housing in Africa, including land tenure issues, high construction costs, limited access to finance, and inadequate urban planning. "Addressing the affordable housing crisis requires a multi-faceted approach that addresses both supply and demand-side factors," Ms. Nkrumah said. "Governments, developers, and civil society organizations must work together to implement policies, programs, and initiatives that increase access to affordable housing for all."

To provide a tangible example, Ms. Nkrumah arranged for Alex to visit a low-income housing project underway in a peri-urban area. They toured the construction site, met with residents, and learned about the innovative financing mechanisms and community engagement strategies being employed to make homeownership more accessible to low-income families.

"As urban populations continue to grow and economies expand, the demand for affordable housing is only going to increase," Ms. Nkrumah explained. "It's imperative that we invest in scalable and sustainable solutions that address the housing needs of all segments of society, from low-income families to middle-income earners."

As they delved deeper into the discussion, Ms. Nkrumah emphasized the importance of adopting a people-centered approach to affordable housing initiatives that prioritizes inclusivity, dignity, and community participation. "Affordable housing is not just about building structures; it's about creating vibrant, resilient, and inclusive communities where people can thrive and prosper," she said. "By involving residents in the design, planning, and management of housing projects, we can ensure that their needs and aspirations are met and that housing solutions are tailored to the unique context and culture of each community."

Later that afternoon, Ms. Nkrumah arranged for Alex to attend a workshop on affordable housing initiatives in Africa. The workshop brought together government officials, housing developers, financial institutions, and civil society organizations to discuss best practices, innovative financing models, and policy frameworks for increasing access to affordable housing across the continent.

Alex found the workshop enlightening, gaining valuable insights into the diverse approaches and partnerships being leveraged to address the affordable housing crisis in Africa. He was impressed by the commitment and collaboration of stakeholders from across sectors to finding sustainable solutions to the housing challenges facing the continent.

As the day came to a close, Alex thanked Ms. Nkrumah for her insights and hospitality. He left her office feeling more informed and inspired than ever to explore opportunities for affordable housing initiatives in Africa, knowing that housing was not just a basic need but a fundamental human right that could transform lives and communities.

Back at his hotel, Alex reflected on the day's discussions. Affordable housing initiatives in Africa were not just about providing shelter; they were about empowering people, reducing poverty, and building more inclusive and sustainable cities. Armed with this understanding, he felt ready to contribute to the efforts to address the affordable housing crisis in Africa, knowing that the solutions he supported would have a lasting impact on the lives of millions of people across the continent.

9.4: Investment in Smart Cities

As the day progressed, Alex delved into the transformative potential of investment in smart cities, recognizing the opportunities they present for sustainable urban development in Africa. His next meeting awaited him with Mr. Kwame Mensah, a visionary urban planner renowned for his expertise in leveraging technology to create smart and sustainable cities.

Mr. Mensah welcomed Alex into his office, a space adorned with futuristic city models, digital screens displaying urban analytics, and interactive maps showcasing innovative urban solutions. "Good afternoon, Alex," he greeted warmly. "Today, we'll explore the exciting prospects of investment in smart cities and their potential to revolutionize urban living in Africa."

Eager to learn, Alex settled into his seat as Mr. Mensah began to elucidate the intricacies of smart cities. "Smart cities leverage digital technologies, data analytics, and connectivity to enhance the efficiency, sustainability, and quality of urban life," he explained. "They integrate smart infrastructure, such as sensors, IoT devices, and real-time monitoring systems, to optimize resource usage, improve service delivery, and enhance the overall urban experience."

He highlighted the key benefits and components of smart cities, emphasizing their potential to address pressing urban challenges, such as traffic congestion, air pollution, and resource scarcity. "Investment in smart cities offers a unique opportunity to leapfrog traditional development models and build more resilient, inclusive, and sustainable urban environments," Mr. Mensah said. "By harnessing the power of technology and innovation, cities can become more livable, competitive, and responsive to the needs of residents and businesses."

To provide a tangible example, Mr. Mensah arranged for Alex to visit a smart city pilot project underway in a rapidly growing urban area. They toured smart buildings, connected infrastructure, and digital public services, witnessing firsthand the transformative impact of technology on urban living.

"As urban populations continue to grow and economies evolve, the demand for smart solutions is only going to increase," Mr. Mensah explained. "It's imperative that we invest in smart infrastructure, digital platforms, and data-driven policies that empower cities to become more resilient, efficient, and sustainable in the face of urbanization."

As they delved deeper into the discussion, Mr. Mensah emphasized the importance of collaboration, innovation, and citizen engagement in driving the development of smart cities. "Smart cities are not just about technology; they're about people," he said. "By involving residents, businesses, and other stakeholders in the design, planning, and implementation of smart initiatives, we can ensure that smart cities are inclusive, equitable, and responsive to the needs of all."

Later that afternoon, Mr. Mensah arranged for Alex to attend a symposium on smart city investment in Africa. The symposium brought together technology companies, urban planners, policymakers, and investors to discuss best practices, case studies, and investment opportunities in smart city development across the continent.

Alex found the symposium enlightening, gaining valuable insights into the transformative potential of smart city investment in Africa. He was impressed by the innovative solutions and partnerships being forged to address urban challenges and improve the quality of life for residents, as well as the role of technology and data in driving sustainable urban development.

As the day came to a close, Alex thanked Mr. Mensah for his insights and hospitality. He left his office feeling more informed and inspired than ever to explore opportunities for investment in smart cities in Africa, knowing that smart solutions would be key to unlocking the full potential of urbanization and driving sustainable growth and prosperity for all stakeholders involved.

Back at his hotel, Alex reflected on the day's discussions.

Investment in smart cities was not just about building infrastructure; it was about harnessing the power of technology and innovation to create more livable, resilient, and inclusive urban environments. Armed with this understanding, he felt ready to contribute to the efforts to build smart cities in Africa, knowing that the solutions he supported would have a lasting impact on the future of urban living on the continent.

9.5: Regulatory and Market Dynamics

As the day progressed, Alex delved into the intricate regulatory and market dynamics shaping real estate and urban development in Africa, recognizing their profound impact on investment opportunities and project viability. His next meeting awaited him with Ms. Fatoumata Diop, a seasoned real estate lawyer renowned for her expertise in navigating regulatory frameworks and market trends across the continent.

Ms. Diop welcomed Alex into her office, a space adorned with legal documents, regulatory statutes, and market analysis reports. "Good afternoon, Alex," she greeted warmly. "Today, we'll explore the complex interplay between regulatory frameworks and market dynamics in African real estate and urban development."

Eager to learn, Alex settled into his seat as Ms. Diop began to elucidate the intricacies of regulatory and market dynamics. "Real estate development in Africa is subject to a myriad of regulatory requirements, land tenure systems, and market forces that vary significantly from one country to another," she explained. "Understanding these complexities is essential for investors and developers looking to navigate the legal and business landscape of real estate in Africa."

She highlighted the key regulatory frameworks and market dynamics affecting real estate and urban development, emphasizing the importance of due diligence, compliance, and risk management in mitigating legal and financial uncertainties. "Regulatory frameworks encompass land use planning, zoning regulations, environmental assessments, construction permits, and property rights, among others," Ms. Diop said. "Navigating these frameworks requires a deep understanding of local laws, regulations, and administrative procedures, as well as effective stakeholder engagement and advocacy."

To provide a tangible example, Ms. Diop arranged for Alex to attend a seminar on land tenure systems in Africa. The seminar brought together legal experts, policymakers, and community leaders to discuss the complexities of land ownership, land rights, and customary land tenure systems across the continent.

"As urbanization accelerates and demand for real estate grows, the need for clear and transparent regulatory frameworks becomes increasingly critical," Ms. Diop explained. "Investors and developers must work closely with governments, communities, and other stakeholders to advocate for regulatory reforms that promote sustainable development, protect property rights, and foster a conducive business environment."

As they delved deeper into the discussion, Ms. Diop emphasized the importance of market dynamics, such as supply and demand, economic trends, and investor sentiment, in shaping real estate investment decisions. "Market dynamics influence property prices, rental yields, occupancy rates, and investment returns," she said. "Investors and developers must conduct thorough market analysis and feasibility studies to assess the potential risks and opportunities of real estate projects in Africa."

Later that afternoon, Ms. Diop arranged for Alex to meet with a panel of industry experts to discuss market trends and investment opportunities in African real estate. The panel provided valuable insights into emerging sectors, growth markets, and innovative financing models for real estate development across the continent.

Alex found the discussion enlightening, gaining valuable insights into the regulatory and market dynamics shaping real estate and urban development in Africa. He was impressed by the depth and breadth of knowledge shared by the panelists and the importance of legal and market expertise in driving successful real estate projects.

As the day came to a close, Alex thanked Ms. Diop for her insights and hospitality. He left her office feeling more informed and empowered than ever to navigate the complex regulatory and market landscape of real estate in Africa, knowing that a deep understanding of these dynamics would be instrumental in identifying and seizing investment opportunities in the dynamic and evolving markets of the continent.

Back at his hotel, Alex reflected on the day's discussions. Regulatory and market dynamics were not just challenges to overcome; they were opportunities to innovate, collaborate, and create value in African real estate and urban development. Armed with this understanding, he felt ready to embark on his journey of exploring investment opportunities in Africa, knowing that the strategies and insights he gained would be crucial in driving success and prosperity in the dynamic and competitive business landscape of the continent.

9.6: Summary and Conclusion

As the sun dipped below the horizon, casting a warm glow over the bustling city streets, Alex reflected on the wealth of knowledge and insights he had gained throughout his exploration of real estate and urban development in Africa. With the day drawing to a close, he sat down to summarize his learnings and draw conclusions from his experiences.

Taking out his notebook, Alex began to jot down his thoughts, distilling the complexities of real estate and urban development into concise points. "Real estate in Africa is a dynamic and multifaceted sector," he wrote, "shaped by a complex interplay of regulatory frameworks, market dynamics, and socio-economic factors."

He reflected on the diverse range of topics he had explored throughout the day, from affordable housing initiatives to investment in smart cities, recognizing the importance of addressing pressing urban challenges while capitalizing on emerging opportunities. "Affordable housing is a pressing need," he noted, "requiring innovative solutions and collaborative efforts to increase access to safe, decent, and affordable housing for all."

As he continued to write, Alex emphasized the transformative potential of investment in smart cities, highlighting their ability to enhance the efficiency, sustainability, and quality of urban life. "Smart cities offer a unique opportunity to leverage technology and innovation," he wrote, "to create vibrant, resilient, and inclusive urban environments that foster economic growth and improve the well-being of residents."

Turning his attention to regulatory and market dynamics, Alex acknowledged the complexities and challenges of navigating legal frameworks and market forces in African real estate. "Understanding regulatory and market dynamics is essential," he wrote, "for investors and developers to mitigate risks, seize opportunities, and drive successful real estate projects."

As he concluded his summary, Alex reflected on the rich tapestry of experiences and insights he had gathered throughout the day. "Real estate and urban development in Africa are dynamic and evolving," he wrote, "requiring creativity, collaboration, and innovation to unlock their full potential and drive sustainable growth and prosperity for all."

With a sense of satisfaction, Alex closed his notebook, knowing that his journey of exploration had only just begun. As he prepared to embark on the next chapter of his adventure, he felt a renewed sense of purpose and determination, knowing that the knowledge and insights he had gained would serve him well in his pursuit of opportunities in African real estate and urban development.

As the city lights flickered to life outside his window, Alex looked forward to the challenges and opportunities that lay ahead, knowing that with passion, perseverance, and a deep understanding of the complexities of real estate and urban development in Africa, he could make a meaningful impact and contribute to the growth and prosperity of the continent.

10

Chapter 10: Financial Services and Banking

10.1: Overview of Africa's Financial Sector

As the morning sun illuminated the bustling streets, Alex delved into the vibrant world of financial services and banking in Africa, recognizing the pivotal role they play in driving economic growth and development on the continent. His journey began with a meeting with Mr. Adeoluwa Babatunde, a seasoned banker renowned for his expertise in navigating the diverse landscape of Africa's financial sector.

Mr. Babatunde welcomed Alex into his office, a space adorned with charts, graphs, and financial reports depicting the dynamic evolution of Africa's financial markets. "Good morning, Alex," he greeted warmly. "Today, we'll explore the multifaceted world of financial services and banking in Africa and the opportunities they present for investors and entrepreneurs."

CHAPTER 10: FINANCIAL SERVICES AND BANKING

Eager to learn, Alex settled into his seat as Mr. Babatunde began to elucidate the intricacies of Africa's financial sector. "The financial sector in Africa is diverse and dynamic, encompassing a wide range of institutions, products, and services," he explained. "From traditional banks and microfinance institutions to fintech startups and mobile money platforms, the sector is evolving rapidly to meet the diverse needs of consumers and businesses across the continent."

He highlighted the key trends and characteristics of Africa's financial sector, emphasizing the importance of understanding local market dynamics, regulatory frameworks, and technological innovations. "Africa's financial sector is characterized by innovation, resilience, and adaptability," Mr. Babatunde said. "Despite facing challenges such as limited access to finance, regulatory constraints, and infrastructure gaps, the sector has continued to grow and expand, driven by factors such as demographic shifts, urbanization, and technological advancements."

To provide a tangible example, Mr. Babatunde arranged for Alex to visit a bustling financial district in a major African city. They toured banks, insurance companies, stock exchanges, and fintech hubs, witnessing firsthand the vibrancy and diversity of Africa's financial ecosystem.

"As economies grow and societies evolve, the demand for financial services is on the rise," Mr. Babatunde explained. "From basic banking services such as savings accounts and loans to more sophisticated products such as insurance, investments, and digital payments, financial services are essential for promoting economic inclusion, empowering individuals, and fostering entrepreneurship and innovation."

As they delved deeper into the discussion, Mr. Babatunde

emphasized the importance of leveraging technology and innovation to expand access to financial services and drive financial inclusion in Africa. "Technology has the power to revolutionize the way financial services are delivered and consumed," he said. "From mobile banking and digital payments to blockchain and artificial intelligence, technology is enabling new business models, improving efficiency, and reducing costs in the financial sector."

Later that morning, Mr. Babatunde arranged for Alex to attend a conference on fintech innovation in Africa. The conference brought together industry experts, entrepreneurs, policymakers, and investors to discuss the latest trends, challenges, and opportunities in Africa's fintech landscape.

Alex found the conference enlightening, gaining valuable insights into the transformative potential of fintech innovation in Africa. He was impressed by the creativity and ingenuity of entrepreneurs and startups in developing innovative solutions to address the unique challenges of Africa's financial sector, as well as the role of regulation and collaboration in fostering a conducive environment for fintech growth and innovation.

As the conference came to a close, Alex thanked Mr. Babatunde for his insights and hospitality. He left the conference feeling inspired and invigorated, knowing that the knowledge and insights he had gained would be instrumental in understanding the complexities and opportunities of Africa's financial sector.

Back at his hotel, Alex reflected on the day's discussions. Africa's financial sector was not just a sector of numbers and transactions; it was a sector of innovation and opportunity, driving economic growth, empowering individuals, and transforming societies. Armed with this understanding, he felt ready to explore opportunities in Africa's financial sector, knowing that the insights and connections he had gained would be invaluable in navigating the dynamic and evolving landscape of finance on the continent.

10.2: Banking and Microfinance

As the morning sun continued to illuminate the cityscape, Alex delved deeper into the intricate world of banking and microfinance in Africa, recognizing their crucial role in driving financial inclusion and economic empowerment across the continent. His exploration led him to a meeting with Ms. Amina Ndiaye, a seasoned banker with extensive experience in both traditional banking and microfinance operations in Africa.

Ms. Ndiaye greeted Alex warmly as he entered her office, which exuded an air of professionalism and efficiency. "Good morning, Alex," she said with a smile. "Today, we'll delve into the fascinating realm of banking and microfinance in Africa and their profound impact on the lives of individuals and communities."

Eager to learn, Alex settled into his seat as Ms. Ndiaye began to elucidate the intricacies of banking and microfinance. "Banking and microfinance are essential pillars of Africa's financial ecosystem, providing individuals and businesses with access to essential financial services," she explained. "While traditional banks cater to the needs of large corporations and high-net-worth individuals, microfinance institutions specialize in serving the financial needs of underserved and marginalized communities, including smallholder farmers, entrepreneurs, and women-led enterprises."

She highlighted the key role that banks and microfinance institutions play in promoting financial inclusion, empowering individuals, and fostering economic development in Africa. "Access to basic financial services such as savings accounts, loans, and insurance is critical for enabling individuals to invest in education, healthcare, and entrepreneurship, thereby improving their livelihoods and lifting themselves out of poverty," Ms. Ndiaye said.

To provide a tangible example, Ms. Ndiaye arranged for Alex to visit a bustling microfinance institution in a peri-urban area. They met with loan officers, visited small businesses that had benefited from microloans, and spoke with borrowers who shared their stories of how access to finance had transformed their lives and livelihoods.

"As economies evolve and societies progress, the demand for banking and microfinance services is only going to increase," Ms. Ndiaye explained. "From rural villages to urban slums, individuals and businesses across Africa are seeking access to financial services that meet their unique needs and circumstances."

As they delved deeper into the discussion, Ms. Ndiaye emphasized the importance of innovation and technology in expanding access to banking and microfinance services in Africa. "Mobile banking, digital payments, and agent banking are revolutionizing the way financial services are delivered and consumed in Africa," she said. "By leveraging technology and partnerships, banks and microfinance institutions can reach more customers, reduce costs, and improve the efficiency and effectiveness of their operations."

Later that morning, Ms. Ndiaye arranged for Alex to attend a workshop on innovative banking solutions in Africa. The workshop brought together bankers, fintech entrepreneurs, policymakers, and development practitioners to discuss best practices, challenges, and opportunities in leveraging technology to enhance banking and microfinance services in Africa.

Alex found the workshop enlightening, gaining valuable insights into the transformative potential of innovative banking solutions in Africa. He was impressed by the creativity and ingenuity of entrepreneurs and practitioners in developing solutions that addressed the unique challenges of banking and microfinance in Africa, as well as the importance of collaboration and partnerships in driving innovation and expanding access to financial services across the continent.

As the workshop came to a close, Alex thanked Ms. Ndiaye for her insights and hospitality. He left her office feeling inspired and energized, knowing that the knowledge and connections he had gained would be invaluable in understanding the complexities and opportunities of banking and microfinance in Africa.

Back at his hotel, Alex reflected on the day's discussions. Banking and microfinance were not just about financial transactions; they were about empowering individuals, fostering entrepreneurship, and driving economic growth and development across Africa. Armed with this understanding, he felt ready to explore opportunities in banking and microfinance, knowing that the insights and connections he had gained would be instrumental in navigating the dynamic and evolving landscape of finance on the continent.

10.3: Capital Markets and Stock Exchanges

As the morning sun continued its ascent, Alex's exploration of Africa's financial sector led him deeper into the realm of capital markets and stock exchanges, where investment opportunities and economic growth intersect. His journey brought him to a meeting with Mr. Ibrahim Diallo, a seasoned investment banker with a wealth of experience in navigating Africa's capital markets and stock exchanges.

Mr. Diallo welcomed Alex into his office, a space adorned with financial charts, market analyses, and news updates from around the world. "Good morning, Alex," he greeted warmly. "Today, we'll delve into the dynamic world of capital markets and stock exchanges in Africa and their role in driving investment, growth, and development across the continent."

Eager to learn, Alex settled into his seat as Mr. Diallo began to elucidate the intricacies of capital markets and stock exchanges. "Capital markets play a crucial role in mobilizing savings, allocating capital, and facilitating investment in productive enterprises," he explained. "Stock exchanges serve as platforms for buying and selling securities, providing companies with access to capital and investors with opportunities for wealth creation and portfolio diversification."

He highlighted the key functions and benefits of capital markets and stock exchanges, emphasizing their ability to facilitate economic growth, spur innovation, and foster entrepreneurship in Africa. "Capital markets enable companies to raise funds for expansion, research and development, and new ventures, thereby fueling economic activity and creating jobs," Mr. Diallo said.

To provide a tangible example, Mr. Diallo arranged for Alex

to visit a bustling stock exchange in a major African city. They observed traders, brokers, and investors in action, witnessing the excitement and energy of the trading floor as stocks were bought and sold, and prices fluctuated in response to market dynamics.

"As economies mature and financial systems develop, the importance of capital markets and stock exchanges grows," Mr. Diallo explained. "From initial public offerings (IPOs) and bond issuances to secondary market trading and corporate governance, capital markets play a vital role in allocating resources efficiently and promoting transparency and accountability in corporate governance."

As they delved deeper into the discussion, Mr. Diallo emphasized the importance of regulatory frameworks, investor confidence, and market infrastructure in fostering vibrant and resilient capital markets in Africa. "Regulatory oversight, investor protection, and market transparency are essential for maintaining the integrity and stability of capital markets," he said.

Later that morning, Mr. Diallo arranged for Alex to attend a seminar on investment opportunities in Africa's capital markets. The seminar brought together investment bankers, fund managers, analysts, and regulators to discuss emerging trends, opportunities, and challenges in Africa's capital markets.

Alex found the seminar enlightening, gaining valuable insights into the diverse range of investment opportunities available in Africa's capital markets, from equities and bonds to derivatives and alternative investments. He was impressed by the depth and breadth of knowledge shared by the speakers and the potential for capital markets to drive economic growth and development across the continent.

As the seminar came to a close, Alex thanked Mr. Diallo for his insights and hospitality. He left his office feeling inspired and energized, knowing that the knowledge and connections he had gained would be invaluable in understanding the complexities and opportunities of capital markets and stock exchanges in Africa.

Back at his hotel, Alex reflected on the day's discussions. Capital markets and stock exchanges were not just about buying and selling securities; they were about mobilizing capital, allocating resources, and driving economic transformation across Africa. Armed with this understanding, he felt ready to explore opportunities in Africa's capital markets, knowing that the insights and connections he had gained would be instrumental in navigating the dynamic and evolving landscape of finance on the continent.

10.4: Insurance and Pension Funds

As the day progressed, Alex's exploration of Africa's financial sector led him to delve into the vital realms of insurance and pension funds, crucial pillars of financial security and stability for individuals and societies alike. His journey continued with a meeting arranged by Ms. Fatou Mbengue, a seasoned actuary with extensive experience in the insurance and pension industries in Africa.

Ms. Mbengue welcomed Alex into her office, a space adorned with charts, graphs, and demographic data depicting the intricate workings of insurance and pension systems across the continent. "Good afternoon, Alex," she greeted warmly. "Today, we'll explore the fundamental role of insurance and pension funds in safeguarding the financial well-being of individuals and communities in Africa."

Eager to learn, Alex settled into his seat as Ms. Mbengue began to elucidate the intricacies of insurance and pension funds. "Insurance provides individuals and businesses with protection against various risks, including accidents, illness, property damage, and loss of income," she explained. "Pension funds, on the other hand, enable individuals to save for retirement and ensure financial security in old age."

She highlighted the key functions and benefits of insurance and pension funds, emphasizing their ability to mitigate risks, provide financial security, and promote long-term savings and investment in Africa. "Insurance and pension funds play a crucial role in promoting economic stability and social welfare," Ms. Mbengue said. "By pooling risks and resources, they enable individuals and societies to cope with unforeseen events and plan for the future with confidence."

To provide a tangible example, Ms. Mbengue arranged for Alex to visit a bustling insurance company and pension fund office in a major African city. They met with insurance agents, pension advisors, and policyholders, witnessing firsthand the importance of insurance and pension funds in providing peace of mind and financial security to individuals and families.

"As economies grow and societies evolve, the demand for insurance and pension services is on the rise," Ms. Mbengue explained. "From life and health insurance to property and casualty insurance, individuals and businesses across Africa are seeking protection against a wide range of risks."

As they delved deeper into the discussion, Ms. Mbengue emphasized the importance of innovation, regulation, and consumer education in advancing the insurance and pension industries in Africa. "Innovative products, such as microinsurance and index-based insurance, are expanding access to insurance services for underserved populations," she said. "Regulatory oversight and consumer protection measures are essential for ensuring the integrity and solvency of insurance companies and pension funds."

Later that afternoon, Ms. Mbengue arranged for Alex to attend a seminar on retirement planning and insurance literacy in Africa. The seminar brought together insurance professionals, pension experts, policymakers, and consumer advocates to discuss best practices, challenges, and opportunities in promoting financial literacy and retirement preparedness across the continent.

Alex found the seminar enlightening, gaining valuable insights into the importance of insurance and pension literacy in empowering individuals to make informed financial decisions and plan for their futures. He was impressed by the efforts of stakeholders to raise awareness about the importance of insurance and pension savings and the potential for insurance and pension funds to drive economic growth and social development in Africa.

As the seminar came to a close, Alex thanked Ms. Mbengue for her insights and hospitality. He left her office feeling inspired and empowered, knowing that the knowledge and connections he had gained would be invaluable in understanding the complexities and opportunities of insurance and pension funds in Africa.

Back at his hotel, Alex reflected on the day's discussions. Insurance and pension funds were not just about financial products; they were about peace of mind, financial security, and long-term planning for individuals and societies in Africa.

Armed with this understanding, he felt ready to explore opportunities in insurance and pension funds, knowing that the insights and connections he had gained would be instrumental in navigating the dynamic and evolving landscape of finance on the continent.

10.5: Investment in Financial Technology

As the day progressed, Alex's exploration of Africa's financial sector took him into the exciting realm of financial technology, where innovation and digitalization are transforming the way financial services are delivered and accessed across the continent. His journey continued with a meeting arranged by Mr. Kwame Amoah, a visionary entrepreneur and fintech enthusiast at the forefront of Africa's digital finance revolution.

Mr. Amoah welcomed Alex into his office, a space buzzing with energy and creativity, adorned with posters and screens showcasing the latest fintech innovations and startups in Africa. "Good afternoon, Alex," he greeted enthusiastically. "Today, we'll dive into the dynamic world of financial technology in Africa and the transformative impact it's having on the financial landscape."

Eager to learn, Alex settled into his seat as Mr. Amoah began to elucidate the intricacies of fintech in Africa. "Financial technology, or fintech, encompasses a wide range of innovative solutions and services that leverage technology to enhance financial processes, products, and services," he explained. "From mobile banking and digital payments to peer-to-peer lending and robo-advisors, fintech is revolutionizing the way financial services are accessed and consumed in Africa."

He highlighted the key trends and drivers of fintech growth

in Africa, emphasizing the role of technology, entrepreneurship, and regulatory innovation in driving innovation and adoption. "Africa's fintech ecosystem is booming," Mr. Amoah said. "Driven by factors such as mobile penetration, internet connectivity, and a young and tech-savvy population, fintech startups are disrupting traditional financial services and expanding access to finance for millions of Africans."

To provide a tangible example, Mr. Amoah arranged for Alex to visit a bustling fintech hub in a major African city. They toured coworking spaces, innovation labs, and startup incubators, meeting with entrepreneurs, developers, and investors who were driving fintech innovation and entrepreneurship across the continent.

"As economies digitize and financial systems evolve, the demand for fintech solutions is only going to increase," Mr. Amoah explained. "From financial inclusion and access to credit to investment management and risk mitigation, fintech is addressing some of the most pressing challenges in Africa's financial sector and unlocking new opportunities for growth and prosperity."

As they delved deeper into the discussion, Mr. Amoah emphasized the importance of collaboration, regulation, and talent development in advancing fintech innovation in Africa. "Partnerships between fintech startups, traditional financial institutions, and regulatory authorities are essential for fostering a conducive ecosystem for fintech growth and innovation," he said.

Later that afternoon, Mr. Amoah arranged for Alex to attend a pitch event showcasing some of the most promising fintech startups in Africa. The event brought together investors, venture capitalists, and industry experts to discover and support the next generation of fintech innovators.

Alex found the event inspiring, gaining valuable insights into the diversity and creativity of fintech solutions emerging in Africa. He was impressed by the passion and vision of the entrepreneurs pitching their ideas and the potential for fintech to drive financial inclusion, innovation, and economic development across the continent.

As the event came to a close, Alex thanked Mr. Amoah for his insights and hospitality. He left the event feeling inspired and energized, knowing that the knowledge and connections he had gained would be invaluable in understanding the complexities and opportunities of fintech investment in Africa.

Back at his hotel, Alex reflected on the day's discussions. Fintech was not just about technology; it was about empowerment, inclusion, and opportunity for millions of Africans. Armed with this understanding, he felt ready to explore opportunities in fintech investment, knowing that the insights and connections he had gained would be instrumental in navigating the dynamic and evolving landscape of finance on the continent.

10.6: Summary and Conclusion

As the sun began to set on the horizon, Alex reflected on the wealth of knowledge and insights he had gained throughout his exploration of Africa's financial sector. With the day drawing to a close, he sat down to summarize his learnings and draw conclusions from his experiences.

Taking out his notebook, Alex began to jot down his thoughts, distilling the complexities of financial services and banking in Africa into concise points. "Financial services and banking in Africa are dynamic and multifaceted," he wrote, "shaped by innovation, technology, and a rapidly evolving regulatory landscape."

He reflected on the diverse range of topics he had explored throughout the day, from traditional banking and microfinance to insurance, pension funds, and fintech innovation. "Access to financial services is essential for driving economic growth, empowering individuals, and fostering entrepreneurship and innovation," he noted.

As he continued to write, Alex emphasized the transformative potential of financial technology in Africa, highlighting its ability to expand access to finance, enhance efficiency, and promote inclusion and innovation. "Fintech is revolutionizing the way financial services are delivered and accessed," he wrote, "unlocking new opportunities for growth and prosperity across the continent."

Turning his attention to the future, Alex recognized the importance of collaboration, regulation, and talent development in advancing Africa's financial sector. "Partnerships between traditional financial institutions, fintech startups, and regulatory authorities are essential for fostering a conducive ecosystem for innovation and growth," he said.

As he concluded his summary, Alex reflected on the rich tapestry of experiences and insights he had gathered throughout the day. "Financial services and banking in Africa are not just about transactions and products," he wrote, "but about empowerment, inclusion, and opportunity for millions of Africans."

With a sense of satisfaction, Alex closed his notebook, knowing that his journey of exploration had only just begun. As he prepared to embark on the next chapter of his adventure, he felt a renewed sense of purpose and determination, knowing that the knowledge and insights he had gained would serve him well in his pursuit of opportunities in Africa's financial sector.

As the city lights flickered to life outside his window, Alex looked forward to the challenges and opportunities that lay ahead, knowing that with passion, perseverance, and a deep understanding of the complexities of financial services and banking in Africa, he could make a meaningful impact and contribute to the growth and prosperity of the continent.

11

Chapter 11: The Role of Foreign Direct Investment (FDI)

11.1: Trends in FDI in Africa

As dawn broke over the African horizon, Alex's exploration of the continent's economic landscape led him to delve into the pivotal role of Foreign Direct Investment (FDI) in driving growth and development across Africa. His journey continued with a meeting arranged by Dr. Aisha Kamara, a renowned economist specializing in FDI trends and analysis in Africa.

Dr. Kamara greeted Alex with a warm smile as he entered her office, a space adorned with maps, charts, and data visualizations depicting the complex patterns of FDI flows into Africa. "Good morning, Alex," she said. "Today, we'll explore the dynamic world of Foreign Direct Investment in Africa and the trends shaping its trajectory across the continent."

Eager to learn, Alex settled into his seat as Dr. Kamara began to elucidate the intricacies of FDI in Africa. "Foreign

Direct Investment plays a crucial role in driving economic growth, stimulating productivity, and promoting innovation and technology transfer in Africa," she explained. "From multinational corporations to sovereign wealth funds and private equity firms, foreign investors bring capital, expertise, and market access that can help unlock the continent's vast potential."

She highlighted the key trends and drivers of FDI in Africa, emphasizing the continent's growing attractiveness as an investment destination and the diversification of FDI sources and sectors. "Africa's investment landscape is evolving rapidly," Dr. Kamara said. "Driven by factors such as demographic trends, urbanization, natural resource endowments, and policy reforms, FDI inflows into Africa have surged in recent years, reflecting the continent's rising prominence on the global stage."

To provide a tangible example, Dr. Kamara arranged for Alex to visit a bustling industrial park in a major African city, where multinational corporations from around the world had set up operations to capitalize on Africa's growing consumer markets and abundant natural resources. They toured factories, research labs, and production facilities, witnessing firsthand the impact of FDI on job creation, skills development, and technology transfer.

"As economies diversify and value chains globalize, the role of FDI in Africa is becoming increasingly important," Dr. Kamara explained. "From manufacturing and services to agriculture and infrastructure, FDI is driving investment and innovation across a wide range of sectors, fueling economic growth and creating opportunities for local businesses and communities."

As they delved deeper into the discussion, Dr. Kamara emphasized the importance of policy coherence, investment promotion, and regulatory reform in attracting and maximizing the benefits of FDI in Africa. "Governments play a critical role in creating an enabling environment for FDI," she said. "By implementing sound macroeconomic policies, improving infrastructure, strengthening institutions, and enhancing the ease of doing business, African countries can attract more FDI and ensure that it contributes to sustainable and inclusive development."

Later that morning, Dr. Kamara arranged for Alex to attend a seminar on FDI trends and opportunities in Africa. The seminar brought together policymakers, business leaders, academics, and investors to discuss best practices, challenges, and strategies for promoting FDI in Africa.

Alex found the seminar enlightening, gaining valuable insights into the diverse range of FDI opportunities available in Africa and the importance of collaboration and partnership in driving sustainable and inclusive investment growth. He was impressed by the commitment of stakeholders to harnessing the potential of FDI to drive economic transformation and improve the lives of people across the continent.

As the seminar came to a close, Alex thanked Dr. Kamara for her insights and hospitality. He left her office feeling inspired and energized, knowing that the knowledge and connections he had gained would be invaluable in understanding the complexities and opportunities of FDI in Africa.

Back at his hotel, Alex reflected on the day's discussions. Foreign Direct Investment was not just about capital inflows; it was about driving growth, creating jobs, and fostering development across Africa. Armed with this understanding, he felt ready to explore opportunities in FDI, knowing that the insights and connections he had gained would be instrumental in navigating the dynamic and evolving landscape of investment in Africa.

11.2: Key Sources of FDI

As the sun reached its zenith, Alex's journey into the world of Foreign Direct Investment (FDI) in Africa continued with a focus on the key sources driving capital into the continent. This leg of his exploration was facilitated by Mr. Chen Wei, a seasoned investment analyst specializing in FDI trends and patterns across Africa.

Mr. Wei greeted Alex warmly as he entered his office, a space adorned with maps, graphs, and investment reports detailing the flow of capital from around the globe into Africa. "Good afternoon, Alex," he said with a smile. "Today, we'll uncover the diverse array of sources fueling Foreign Direct Investment in Africa and the strategic implications for the continent's economic development."

Eager to delve deeper, Alex settled into his seat as Mr. Wei began to elucidate the intricacies of FDI sources in Africa. "Foreign Direct Investment in Africa comes from a variety of sources, ranging from traditional investors in Europe and North America to emerging markets in Asia and the Middle East," he explained. "Each source brings its own unique strengths, preferences, and motivations, shaping the dynamics of FDI inflows and investment patterns across the continent."

He highlighted the key sources of FDI in Africa, emphasizing the growing role of emerging economies such as China, India, and Brazil, as well as the continued significance of traditional investors from Europe and North America. "China, in particular, has emerged as a major source of FDI in Africa, driven by its strategic interests in natural resources, infrastructure development, and market access," Mr. Wei said.

To provide a tangible example, Mr. Wei arranged for Alex to visit a Chinese-funded infrastructure project in a major African city, where construction was underway on a new highway connecting urban centers and rural communities. They observed engineers, workers, and machinery bustling with activity, a testament to China's investment in Africa's infrastructure and development.

"As Africa's economies grow and diversify, the sources of FDI are also diversifying," Mr. Wei explained. "In addition to traditional sectors such as mining and manufacturing, investors are increasingly exploring opportunities in services, technology, and consumer markets, reflecting the continent's evolving investment landscape and growing middle class."

As they delved deeper into the discussion, Mr. Wei emphasized the importance of understanding the preferences and motivations of different FDI sources in Africa. "Each source of FDI brings its own set of priorities, risk perceptions, and investment strategies," he said. "By understanding these dynamics, African countries can attract and leverage FDI more effectively to drive economic growth and development."

Later that afternoon, Mr. Wei arranged for Alex to attend a roundtable discussion on FDI sourcing strategies in Africa. The discussion brought together government officials, investors, and industry experts to share insights, experiences, and best practices for attracting and maximizing FDI from diverse sources.

Alex found the discussion enlightening, gaining valuable insights into the strategic considerations and challenges involved in attracting FDI from different regions and sectors. He was impressed by the diversity of perspectives and the potential for collaboration and partnership in driving sustainable and inclusive investment growth across Africa.

As the discussion came to a close, Alex thanked Mr. Wei for his insights and hospitality. He left his office feeling inspired and energized, knowing that the knowledge and connections he had gained would be invaluable in understanding the complexities and opportunities of FDI sourcing in Africa.

Back at his hotel, Alex reflected on the day's discussions. Foreign Direct Investment was not just about capital inflows; it was about strategic partnerships, economic diplomacy, and mutual benefit for investors and host countries alike. Armed with this understanding, he felt ready to explore opportunities in FDI sourcing, knowing that the insights and connections he had gained would be instrumental in navigating the dynamic and evolving landscape of investment in Africa.

11.3: Impact of FDI on Economic Development

As the day progressed, Alex's exploration of Foreign Direct Investment (FDI) in Africa deepened, focusing on the transformative impact that capital inflows have on the continent's economic development. This leg of his journey was guided by Dr. Fatima Ndiaye, an esteemed economist renowned for her expertise in analyzing the effects of FDI on African economies.

Dr. Ndiaye welcomed Alex into her office, a space adorned with economic models, charts, and maps illustrating the intricate relationship between FDI and economic development in Africa. "Good afternoon, Alex," she greeted warmly. "Today, we'll explore how Foreign Direct Investment shapes the economic landscape of Africa, driving growth, employment, and structural transformation."

Eager to learn, Alex settled into his seat as Dr. Ndiaye began to elucidate the intricacies of FDI's impact on economic development. "Foreign Direct Investment plays a crucial role in accelerating economic growth, enhancing productivity, and promoting structural transformation in Africa," she explained. "By injecting capital, technology, and expertise into host countries, FDI stimulates investment, creates jobs, and fosters innovation and knowledge transfer."

She highlighted the key channels through which FDI contributes to economic development in Africa, emphasizing its role in driving industrialization, expanding exports, and upgrading infrastructure and technology. "From manufacturing and services to agriculture and infrastructure, FDI spurs investment and innovation across a wide range of sectors, catalyzing economic diversification and competitiveness," Dr. Ndiaye said.

To provide a tangible example, Dr. Ndiaye arranged for Alex to visit a manufacturing plant in a major African city, where a multinational corporation had set up operations to produce consumer electronics for both domestic and export markets. They observed workers assembling products on state-of-the-art production lines, a testament to the transformative impact of FDI on job creation and industrialization in Africa.

"As African economies integrate into global value chains, the impact of FDI becomes even more pronounced," Dr. Ndiaye explained. "By attracting investment from multinational corporations, African countries can leverage their comparative advantages in labor, natural resources, and market access to enhance competitiveness and drive sustainable economic growth."

As they delved deeper into the discussion, Dr. Ndiaye emphasized the importance of policy coherence, investment promotion, and institutional capacity building in maximizing the benefits of FDI for economic development in Africa. "Governments play a critical role in creating an enabling environment for FDI," she said. "By implementing sound macroeconomic policies, improving infrastructure, strengthening institutions, and enhancing the ease of doing business, African countries can attract more FDI and ensure that it contributes to inclusive and sustainable development."

Later that afternoon, Dr. Ndiaye arranged for Alex to attend a conference on FDI and economic development in Africa. The conference brought together policymakers, academics, and business leaders to discuss best practices, challenges, and strategies for leveraging FDI to drive economic transformation and improve livelihoods across the continent.

Alex found the conference enlightening, gaining valuable insights into the complex dynamics of FDI and its impact on African economies. He was impressed by the commitment of stakeholders to harnessing the potential of FDI to drive inclusive and sustainable development, and the potential for collaboration and partnership in maximizing its benefits for host countries and investors alike.

As the conference came to a close, Alex thanked Dr. Ndiaye for her insights and hospitality. He left her office feeling inspired and energized, knowing that the knowledge and connections he had gained would be invaluable in understanding the complexities and opportunities of FDI's impact on economic development in Africa.

Back at his hotel, Alex reflected on the day's discussions. Foreign Direct Investment was not just about capital inflows; it was about driving growth, creating jobs, and fostering structural transformation across Africa. Armed with this understanding, he felt ready to explore opportunities in FDI, knowing that the insights and connections he had gained would be instrumental in navigating the dynamic and evolving landscape of investment in Africa.

11.4: Sectoral Distribution of FDI

As the day unfolded, Alex delved deeper into his exploration of Foreign Direct Investment (FDI) in Africa, focusing now on the sectoral distribution of capital inflows across the continent. This leg of his journey was facilitated by Ms. Amina Diop, a seasoned investment analyst specializing in analyzing the allocation of FDI across different sectors of the economy.

Ms. Diop welcomed Alex into her office, a space adorned with charts, graphs, and economic reports illustrating the diverse array of sectors attracting FDI in Africa. "Good afternoon, Alex," she greeted warmly. "Today, we'll uncover the sectoral distribution of FDI in Africa and explore the strategic implications for economic development and investment opportunities."

Eager to learn, Alex settled into his seat as Ms. Diop began to elucidate the intricacies of sectoral distribution of FDI. "Foreign Direct Investment in Africa is not evenly distributed across sectors," she explained. "Certain industries attract a larger share of capital inflows due to factors such as market size, natural resource endowments, and policy incentives."

She highlighted the key sectors that traditionally attract FDI in Africa, emphasizing industries such as mining, manufacturing, telecommunications, and services. "Natural resource-rich countries often attract significant FDI inflows into the extractive industries, driven by demand for oil, gas, minerals, and other commodities," Ms. Diop said.

To provide a tangible example, Ms. Diop arranged for Alex to visit a mining site in a mineral-rich region of Africa, where multinational corporations had invested heavily in extracting and processing precious metals. They observed miners, engineers, and technicians operating heavy machinery and conducting geological surveys, a testament to the strategic importance of the extractive industries in attracting FDI to Africa.

"As economies diversify and value chains globalize, other sectors such as manufacturing, services, and infrastructure are also attracting significant FDI inflows," Ms. Diop explained. "Investors are drawn to these sectors by factors such as growing consumer markets, urbanization, and infrastructure development, as well as policy incentives and investment promotion efforts."

As they delved deeper into the discussion, Ms. Diop emphasized the importance of understanding the sectoral distribution of FDI in Africa for identifying investment opportunities and informing policy decisions. "By analyzing the patterns and trends of FDI across sectors, policymakers and investors can identify strategic priorities, target high-growth industries, and leverage comparative advantages to attract and maximize the benefits of FDI for economic development," she said.

Later that afternoon, Ms. Diop arranged for Alex to attend a seminar on sectoral trends in FDI in Africa. The seminar brought together government officials, investors, and industry experts to discuss best practices, challenges, and strategies for promoting investment and economic diversification across different sectors of the economy.

Alex found the seminar enlightening, gaining valuable insights into the strategic importance of sectoral distribution of FDI for driving economic growth and development in Africa. He was impressed by the diversity of perspectives and the potential for collaboration and partnership in identifying and capitalizing on investment opportunities across various industries.

As the seminar came to a close, Alex thanked Ms. Diop for her insights and hospitality. He left her office feeling inspired and energized, knowing that the knowledge and connections he had gained would be invaluable in understanding the complexities and opportunities of sectoral distribution of FDI in Africa.

Back at his hotel, Alex reflected on the day's discussions. Foreign Direct Investment was not just about capital inflows; it was about strategic investment decisions, sectoral priorities, and economic diversification across Africa. Armed with this understanding, he felt ready to explore opportunities in FDI, knowing that the insights and connections he had gained would be instrumental in navigating the dynamic and evolving landscape of investment in Africa.

11.5: Policy Framework for Attracting FDI

As the sun began to set, casting a warm glow over the city skyline, Alex's exploration of Foreign Direct Investment (FDI) in Africa continued with a focus on the policy frameworks that shape the continent's attractiveness to investors. This leg of his journey was guided by Mr. Kwame Osei, a respected policy analyst renowned for his expertise in designing and implementing strategies to attract FDI.

Mr. Osei welcomed Alex into his office, a space adorned with policy documents, investment treaties, and economic development plans outlining the initiatives aimed at promoting FDI in Africa. "Good evening, Alex," he greeted with a smile. "Today, we'll explore the critical role of policy frameworks in attracting and maximizing the benefits of Foreign Direct Investment in Africa."

Eager to learn, Alex settled into his seat as Mr. Osei began to elucidate the intricacies of FDI policy frameworks. "The policy environment plays a crucial role in shaping the attractiveness of African countries to foreign investors," he explained. "By implementing sound macroeconomic policies, improving infrastructure, enhancing the ease of doing business, and providing incentives for investment, governments can create an enabling environment that encourages FDI inflows and maximizes their positive impact on economic development."

He highlighted the key components of a conducive policy framework for attracting FDI, emphasizing factors such as political stability, rule of law, property rights protection, and transparency. "Investors are attracted to countries that offer a stable and predictable business environment, where property rights are respected, contracts are enforceable, and regulatory frameworks are transparent and consistent," Mr. Osei said.

To provide a tangible example, Mr. Osei arranged for Alex to meet with government officials responsible for investment promotion in a major African capital. They discussed the various policies and initiatives implemented to attract FDI, including investment incentives, streamlined regulatory processes, and targeted marketing campaigns aimed at showcasing the country's investment opportunities and potential.

"As African countries compete for FDI, the quality of their policy frameworks becomes increasingly important," Mr. Osei explained. "Governments must strive to create an attractive investment climate that addresses the needs and concerns of investors while also ensuring that FDI contributes to sustainable and inclusive development."

As they delved deeper into the discussion, Mr. Osei emphasized the importance of policy coherence, coordination, and stakeholder engagement in designing and implementing effective strategies to attract FDI. "Policymakers must work closely with stakeholders from the public and private sectors to develop policies that address the unique challenges and opportunities of attracting FDI in Africa," he said.

Later that evening, Mr. Osei arranged for Alex to attend a policy dialogue on FDI promotion in Africa. The dialogue brought together government officials, investors, and civil society representatives to discuss best practices, challenges, and strategies for enhancing the policy environment for FDI across the continent.

Alex found the dialogue enlightening, gaining valuable insights into the complex dynamics of FDI policy frameworks and the importance of collaboration and partnership in driving sustainable investment growth in Africa. He was impressed by the commitment of stakeholders to fostering an enabling environment for FDI that promotes economic growth, job creation, and poverty reduction across the continent.

As the dialogue came to a close, Alex thanked Mr. Osei for his insights and hospitality. He left his office feeling inspired and energized, knowing that the knowledge and connections he had gained would be invaluable in understanding the complexities and opportunities of policy frameworks for attracting FDI in Africa.

Back at his hotel, Alex reflected on the day's discussions. Foreign Direct Investment was not just about capital inflows; it was about creating an enabling environment that attracts investors, fosters innovation, and drives sustainable economic growth. Armed with this understanding, he felt ready to explore opportunities in FDI, knowing that the insights and connections he had gained would be instrumental in navigating the dynamic and evolving landscape of investment in Africa.

11.6: Summary and Conclusion

As twilight descended upon the city, casting long shadows across the streets, Alex's journey into the world of Foreign Direct Investment (FDI) in Africa reached its conclusion. Reflecting on the wealth of knowledge and experiences he had gained throughout the day, he felt a sense of fulfillment and enlightenment.

In the quiet of his hotel room, Alex sat down to reflect on the day's discussions, allowing the insights to percolate through his mind like stars emerging in the night sky.

The diverse perspectives and expert guidance he had encountered had illuminated the multifaceted nature of FDI in Africa, from its transformative impact on economic development to the strategic importance of policy frameworks and sectoral priorities.

Through his conversations with economists, analysts, policymakers, and investors, Alex had gained a deeper understanding of the opportunities and challenges of attracting and maximizing the benefits of FDI in Africa.

He had learned how FDI drives growth, fosters innovation, and promotes structural transformation across the continent, unlocking new opportunities for investment and development.

He had discovered the critical role of policy frameworks in creating an enabling environment that attracts investors, fosters innovation, and drives sustainable economic growth.

And he had witnessed firsthand the sectoral distribution of FDI, from the extractive industries to manufacturing, services, and infrastructure, each playing a unique role in shaping Africa's economic landscape.

As he pondered the lessons learned and insights gained, Alex felt a renewed sense of purpose and determination. Foreign Direct Investment was not just about capital inflows; it was about driving growth, creating jobs, and fostering development across Africa.

Armed with this understanding, Alex felt ready to embark on his own journey into the world of investment, knowing that the knowledge and connections he had gained would be invaluable in navigating the dynamic and evolving landscape of FDI in Africa.

As he prepared to bid farewell to the city and continue his exploration of the continent, Alex felt a sense of excitement and anticipation for the opportunities that lay ahead. For in the vast expanse of Africa's economic horizon, he saw endless possibilities for investment, innovation, and growth.

And with each step forward, he knew that he was not just a spectator, but an active participant in shaping the future of Africa's economic destiny.

Chapter 11: The Role of Foreign Direct Investment (FDI)

With a renewed sense of purpose and determination, Alex closed his eyes, ready to embrace the journey that lay ahead, knowing that the adventure had only just begun.

12

Chapter 12: Trade and Regional Integration

12.1: Intra-African Trade and the AfCFTA

As dawn broke over the African horizon, casting a golden hue across the landscape, Alex's exploration into the intricate world of trade and regional integration on the continent began. This leg of his journey was guided by Ms. Aisha Nkosi, a seasoned economist renowned for her expertise in analyzing trade dynamics and regional integration initiatives in Africa.

Ms. Nkosi welcomed Alex into her office, a space adorned with maps, charts, and economic reports detailing the complexities of intra-African trade and the transformative potential of the African Continental Free Trade Area (AfCFTA). "Good morning, Alex," she greeted warmly. "Today, we'll delve into the nuances of intra-African trade and explore the game-changing implications of the AfCFTA for economic integration and development on the continent."

CHAPTER 12: TRADE AND REGIONAL INTEGRATION

Eager to learn, Alex settled into his seat as Ms. Nkosi began to elucidate the intricacies of intra-African trade and the AfCFTA. "Intra-African trade has long been characterized by low levels of integration, hindered by barriers such as tariff barriers, non-tariff barriers, and poor infrastructure," she explained. "However, with the recent establishment of the AfCFTA, Africa is poised to undergo a paradigm shift in trade dynamics, unlocking new opportunities for economic growth, job creation, and poverty reduction."

She highlighted the key objectives of the AfCFTA, emphasizing its potential to create a single market for goods and services, facilitate cross-border trade, and promote regional value chains and industrialization. "By eliminating tariffs on 90% of goods, harmonizing trade rules and regulations, and enhancing infrastructure and connectivity, the AfCFTA aims to boost intra-African trade and foster economic integration, ultimately contributing to the continent's development agenda," Ms. Nkosi said.

To provide a tangible example, Ms. Nkosi arranged for Alex to visit a bustling border post between two African countries, where traders, merchants, and truck drivers were engaged in cross-border commerce. They observed the exchange of goods, currencies, and cultures, a testament to the vibrant and dynamic nature of intra-African trade and the potential for the AfCFTA to further enhance trade facilitation and integration.

"As Africa embarks on its journey towards deeper economic integration, the AfCFTA presents a unique opportunity to harness the continent's vast potential and unlock new pathways for inclusive and sustainable development," Ms. Nkosi explained. "By promoting trade diversification, industrialization, and value addition, the AfCFTA can contribute to job creation, income growth, and poverty reduction, while also enhancing Africa's resilience to external shocks and global economic trends."

As they delved deeper into the discussion, Ms. Nkosi emphasized the importance of policy coordination, infrastructure investment, and stakeholder engagement in realizing the full potential of the AfCFTA. "Governments, businesses, and civil society must work together to address the challenges and seize the opportunities of regional integration," she said. "By fostering a conducive environment for trade and investment, African countries can maximize the benefits of the AfCFTA and build a prosperous and resilient continent for future generations."

Later that morning, Ms. Nkosi arranged for Alex to attend a conference on intra-African trade and the AfCFTA. The conference brought together policymakers, business leaders, and academics to discuss best practices, challenges, and strategies for harnessing the potential of regional integration to drive economic development in Africa.

Alex found the conference enlightening, gaining valuable insights into the transformative potential of the AfCFTA for intra-African trade and regional integration. He was impressed by the commitment of stakeholders to building a more interconnected and prosperous Africa, and the potential for collaboration and partnership in realizing this vision.

As the conference came to a close, Alex thanked Ms. Nkosi for her insights and hospitality. He left her office feeling inspired and energized, knowing that the knowledge and connections he had gained would be invaluable in understanding the complexities and opportunities of trade and regional integration in Africa.

Back at his hotel, Alex reflected on the day's discussions. Trade and regional integration were not just about economic transactions; they were about building bridges, forging partnerships, and unlocking the continent's vast potential. Armed with this understanding, he felt ready to explore opportunities in trade and investment, knowing that the insights and connections he had gained would be instrumental in navigating the dynamic and evolving landscape of Africa's economic integration.

12.2: Trade Policies and Agreements

As the sun climbed higher in the sky, casting a warm glow over the bustling city, Alex's exploration into the realm of trade policies and agreements in Africa continued. This leg of his journey was guided by Mr. Jamal Mbeki, a distinguished trade expert renowned for his insights into the complexities of trade negotiations and agreements on the continent.

Mr. Mbeki welcomed Alex into his office, a space adorned with maps, trade agreements, and policy documents outlining the intricacies of trade policies and their implications for Africa's economic development. "Good day, Alex," he greeted warmly. "Today, we'll delve into the world of trade policies and agreements, exploring their impact on regional integration, economic growth, and development in Africa."

Eager to learn, Alex settled into his seat as Mr. Mbeki began to elucidate the intricacies of trade policies and agreements. "Trade policies and agreements play a crucial role in shaping the dynamics of international trade and investment, influencing market access, competitiveness, and economic development," he explained. "In Africa, a myriad of trade agreements, both regional and international, govern the flow of goods, services, and investments across borders."

He highlighted the key features of trade policies and agreements, emphasizing factors such as tariff rates, rules of origin, customs procedures, and dispute resolution mechanisms. "Trade agreements are designed to facilitate trade and investment by reducing barriers such as tariffs, quotas, and regulatory restrictions," Mr. Mbeki said. "They aim to create a predictable and transparent trading environment that fosters economic integration, competitiveness, and growth."

To provide a tangible example, Mr. Mbeki arranged for Alex to attend a trade negotiation session between African countries, where representatives were engaged in discussions to harmonize trade rules and regulations. They observed diplomats, trade experts, and negotiators deliberating over issues such as tariff harmonization, rules of origin, and market access, a testament to the complex and intricate nature of trade negotiations in Africa.

"As African countries seek to deepen regional integration and expand market access, trade policies and agreements play a pivotal role in shaping the continent's economic future," Mr. Mbeki explained. "By aligning their trade policies and harmonizing their regulations, African countries can create a more conducive environment for trade and investment, unlocking new opportunities for economic growth and development."

As they delved deeper into the discussion, Mr. Mbeki emphasized the importance of capacity building, technical assistance, and institutional strengthening in enhancing Africa's trade negotiation capabilities. "Effective trade negotiations require skilled negotiators, robust institutions, and inclusive stakeholder engagement," he said. "By investing in human capital and institutional capacity, African countries can enhance their ability to negotiate trade agreements that promote their economic interests and contribute to sustainable development."

Later that afternoon, Mr. Mbeki arranged for Alex to attend a seminar on trade policies and agreements in Africa. The seminar brought together government officials, trade experts, and business leaders to discuss best practices, challenges, and strategies for advancing trade negotiations and implementing trade agreements on the continent.

Alex found the seminar enlightening, gaining valuable insights into the complexities of trade policies and agreements and their implications for Africa's economic development. He was impressed by the dedication of stakeholders to fostering a conducive environment for trade and investment, and the potential for collaboration and partnership in advancing Africa's integration into the global economy.

As the seminar came to a close, Alex thanked Mr. Mbeki for his insights and hospitality. He left his office feeling inspired and energized, knowing that the knowledge and connections he had gained would be invaluable in understanding the complexities and opportunities of trade policies and agreements in Africa.

Back at his hotel, Alex reflected on the day's discussions. Trade policies and agreements were not just about regulations and negotiations; they were about building bridges, forging partnerships, and unlocking Africa's vast potential in the global marketplace. Armed with this understanding, he felt ready to explore opportunities in trade and investment, knowing that the insights and connections he had gained would be instrumental in navigating the dynamic and evolving landscape of Africa's economic integration.

12.3: Regional Trade Blocs

As the day wore on, the vibrancy of the city streets mirrored the energy of Alex's exploration into the realm of regional trade blocs in Africa. This leg of his journey was guided by Dr. Fatima Abacha, a renowned economist with expertise in regional integration and trade dynamics across the continent.

Dr. Abacha welcomed Alex into her office, a space adorned with maps, charts, and economic reports illustrating the intricacies of regional trade blocs and their impact on Africa's economic landscape. "Good afternoon, Alex," she greeted warmly. "Today, we'll delve into the world of regional trade blocs, exploring their role in fostering economic integration, trade facilitation, and development in Africa."

Eager to learn, Alex settled into his seat as Dr. Abacha began to elucidate the intricacies of regional trade blocs. "Regional trade blocs are an integral part of Africa's economic architecture, fostering closer economic ties and cooperation among neighboring countries," she explained. "They aim to promote trade, investment, and economic development by reducing barriers to trade, harmonizing regulations, and facilitating cross-border cooperation."

She highlighted the key features of regional trade blocs, emphasizing factors such as tariff liberalization, customs union arrangements, and common market protocols. "Regional trade blocs vary in scope and ambition, ranging from preferential trade agreements to deeper forms of economic integration such as customs unions and common markets," Dr. Abacha said. "Each bloc has its own set of rules, institutions, and objectives, reflecting the unique dynamics and priorities of its member countries."

To provide a tangible example, Dr. Abacha arranged for Alex to visit the headquarters of a regional trade bloc in Africa, where representatives from member countries were engaged in discussions to enhance trade cooperation and integration. They observed diplomats, trade negotiators, and policymakers deliberating over issues such as trade facilitation, infrastructure development, and market access, a testament to the collaborative spirit and shared vision of regional integration in Africa.

"As African countries seek to deepen regional integration and expand market access, regional trade blocs play a pivotal role in shaping the continent's economic future," Dr. Abacha explained. "By promoting trade facilitation, infrastructure development, and policy coordination, regional trade blocs can unlock new opportunities for economic growth and development, while also fostering peace, stability, and cooperation among member countries."

As they delved deeper into the discussion, Dr. Abacha emphasized the importance of inclusive growth, equitable development, and sustainable integration in advancing regional trade blocs in Africa. "Regional integration must be accompanied by policies and initiatives that address the needs and concerns of all stakeholders, including small and medium-sized enterprises, women entrepreneurs, and marginalized communities," she said. "By promoting inclusive growth and equitable development, regional trade blocs can maximize the benefits of integration and ensure that no one is left behind in Africa's journey towards prosperity."

Later that evening, Dr. Abacha arranged for Alex to attend a seminar on regional trade blocs in Africa. The seminar brought together government officials, trade experts, and civil society representatives to discuss best practices, challenges, and strategies for advancing regional integration and cooperation on the continent.

Alex found the seminar enlightening, gaining valuable insights into the complexities of regional trade blocs and their implications for Africa's economic development. He was impressed by the dedication of stakeholders to fostering closer economic ties and cooperation among neighboring countries, and the potential for collaboration and partnership in realizing the vision of a more integrated and prosperous Africa.

As the seminar came to a close, Alex thanked Dr. Abacha for her insights and hospitality. He left her office feeling inspired and energized, knowing that the knowledge and connections he had gained would be invaluable in understanding the complexities and opportunities of regional trade blocs in Africa.

Back at his hotel, Alex reflected on the day's discussions. Regional trade blocs were not just about economic cooperation; they were about building bridges, forging partnerships, and unlocking Africa's vast potential for shared prosperity. Armed with this understanding, he felt ready to explore opportunities in trade and investment, knowing that the insights and connections he had gained would be instrumental in navigating the dynamic and evolving landscape of Africa's economic integration.

12.4: Trade Infrastructure and Logistics

As the day progressed, the city streets buzzed with activity, mirroring the energy of Alex's exploration into the realm of trade infrastructure and logistics in Africa. This leg of his journey was guided by Mr. Ibrahim Sow, a seasoned logistics expert renowned for his insights into the complexities of trade facilitation and infrastructure development across the continent.

Mr. Sow welcomed Alex into his office, a space adorned with maps, shipping manifests, and supply chain diagrams illustrating the intricacies of trade infrastructure and logistics in Africa. "Good afternoon, Alex," he greeted warmly. "Today, we'll delve into the world of trade infrastructure and logistics, exploring their role in facilitating trade, reducing costs, and enhancing competitiveness in Africa."

Eager to learn, Alex settled into his seat as Mr. Sow began to elucidate the intricacies of trade infrastructure and logistics. "Trade infrastructure and logistics are critical enablers of international trade, providing the physical and institutional framework for the efficient movement of goods and services across borders," he explained. "In Africa, inadequate infrastructure and logistical challenges have long been a barrier to trade, hindering economic growth and development."

He highlighted the key components of trade infrastructure and logistics, emphasizing factors such as transport networks, ports, customs procedures, and trade facilitation measures. "Efficient trade infrastructure and logistics are essential for reducing trade costs, improving competitiveness, and enhancing market access," Mr. Sow said. "By investing in infrastructure development, streamlining customs procedures, and adopting best practices in trade facilitation, African countries can unlock new opportunities for trade and economic growth."

To provide a tangible example, Mr. Sow arranged for Alex to visit a major port facility in Africa, where he witnessed the hustle and bustle of cargo handling, container loading, and ship docking operations. They observed port authorities, customs officials, and logistics providers working together to ensure the smooth flow of goods and commodities, a testament to the importance of efficient trade infrastructure and logistics in facilitating international trade.

"As African countries seek to deepen regional integration and expand market access, trade infrastructure and logistics play a pivotal role in shaping the continent's economic future," Mr. Sow explained. "By investing in port modernization, road and rail networks, and trade facilitation measures, African countries can enhance their connectivity, reduce trade costs, and improve their competitiveness in the global marketplace."

As they delved deeper into the discussion, Mr. Sow emphasized the importance of public-private partnerships, technology adoption, and regulatory reforms in advancing trade infrastructure and logistics in Africa. "Efforts to improve trade infrastructure and logistics must be accompanied by policies and initiatives that promote private sector participation, innovation, and efficiency," he said. "By leveraging the expertise and resources of both the public and private sectors, African countries can overcome the challenges of inadequate infrastructure and logistics and unlock the full potential of trade and economic integration."

Later that evening, Mr. Sow arranged for Alex to attend a conference on trade infrastructure and logistics in Africa. The conference brought together government officials, logistics experts, and industry leaders to discuss best practices, challenges, and strategies for advancing trade infrastructure and logistics on the continent.

Alex found the conference enlightening, gaining valuable insights into the complexities of trade infrastructure and logistics and their implications for Africa's economic development. He was impressed by the dedication of stakeholders to improving trade facilitation and infrastructure and the potential for collaboration and partnership in realizing the vision of a more connected and competitive Africa.

As the conference came to a close, Alex thanked Mr. Sow for his insights and hospitality. He left his office feeling inspired and energized, knowing that the knowledge and connections he had gained would be invaluable in understanding the complexities and opportunities of trade infrastructure and logistics in Africa.

Back at his hotel, Alex reflected on the day's discussions. Trade infrastructure and logistics were not just about roads, ports, and warehouses; they were about building bridges, forging partnerships, and unlocking Africa's vast potential for trade and economic growth. Armed with this understanding, he felt ready to explore opportunities in trade and investment, knowing that the insights and connections he had gained would be instrumental in navigating the dynamic and evolving landscape of Africa's economic integration.

12.5: Barriers to Trade and Investment

As the sun dipped below the horizon, casting a golden glow over the city skyline, Alex's exploration into the complexities of trade and regional integration in Africa continued. This leg of his journey was guided by Dr. Amina Diop, a distinguished economist renowned for her expertise in identifying and addressing barriers to trade and investment on the continent.

Dr. Diop welcomed Alex into her office, a space adorned with charts, graphs, and economic reports detailing the myriad challenges facing African economies in their quest for deeper integration and expanded trade. "Good evening, Alex," she greeted warmly. "Today, we'll delve into the world of barriers to trade and investment, exploring the obstacles that hinder economic growth, competitiveness, and development in Africa."

Eager to learn, Alex settled into his seat as Dr. Diop began to elucidate the intricacies of barriers to trade and investment. "Barriers to trade and investment come in many forms, ranging from tariff barriers and non-tariff barriers to regulatory constraints and infrastructure deficiencies," she explained. "In Africa, these barriers have long impeded the flow of goods, services, and capital, hindering economic growth, stifling innovation, and perpetuating poverty."

She highlighted the key barriers to trade and investment, emphasizing factors such as high tariffs, cumbersome customs procedures, weak regulatory frameworks, and inadequate infrastructure. "High trade costs, poor logistics, and regulatory uncertainty deter investors and limit market access, constraining the ability of African businesses to compete globally and stifling the continent's economic potential," Dr. Diop said.

To provide a tangible example, Dr. Diop arranged for Alex to visit a border crossing between two African countries, where he witnessed firsthand the inefficiencies and challenges of cross-border trade. He observed long queues of trucks waiting to clear customs, bureaucratic delays, and cumbersome paperwork, a stark reminder of the barriers that hinder trade and investment in Africa.

"As African countries seek to deepen regional integration and expand market access, addressing barriers to trade and investment is essential for unlocking the continent's economic potential," Dr. Diop explained. "By reducing tariffs, streamlining customs procedures, harmonizing regulations, and investing in infrastructure, African countries can enhance their competitiveness, attract investment, and foster sustainable economic growth."

As they delved deeper into the discussion, Dr. Diop emphasized the importance of policy coordination, institutional reforms, and regional cooperation in addressing barriers to trade and investment in Africa. "Efforts to address barriers to trade and investment must be accompanied by policies and initiatives that promote transparency, accountability, and good governance," she said. "By fostering an enabling environment for trade and investment, African countries can create new opportunities for economic growth, job creation, and poverty reduction."

Later that evening, Dr. Diop arranged for Alex to attend a roundtable discussion on barriers to trade and investment in Africa. The discussion brought together policymakers, business leaders, and civil society representatives to identify challenges, share best practices, and develop strategies for overcoming barriers to trade and investment on the continent.

Alex found the discussion enlightening, gaining valuable insights into the complexities of trade and investment barriers and their implications for Africa's economic development. He was impressed by the commitment of stakeholders to addressing the challenges and unlocking the continent's vast potential for trade and investment.

As the discussion came to a close, Alex thanked Dr. Diop for her insights and hospitality. He left her office feeling inspired and energized, knowing that the knowledge and connections he had gained would be invaluable in understanding the complexities and opportunities of trade and regional integration in Africa.

Back at his hotel, Alex reflected on the day's discussions. Barriers to trade and investment were not just obstacles to be overcome; they were opportunities for collaboration, innovation, and growth. Armed with this understanding, he felt ready to explore opportunities in trade and investment, knowing that the insights and connections he had gained would be instrumental in navigating the dynamic and evolving landscape of Africa's economic integration.

12.7: Summary and Conclusion

As the day drew to a close, Alex found himself reflecting on the myriad complexities and opportunities of trade and regional integration in Africa. Guided by the insights of experts and practitioners, his journey had been enlightening, unveiling the intricate tapestry of challenges and possibilities that shaped the continent's economic landscape.

In the quiet of his hotel room, Alex pulled out his notebook and began to jot down his thoughts. The words flowed effortlessly as he captured the essence of his journey, distilling the key lessons and takeaways that had emerged from his exploration.

"Trade and regional integration are at the heart of Africa's economic transformation," Alex wrote, his pen gliding across the page. "From the bustling markets of Lagos to the bustling ports of Mombasa, the continent pulsates with energy and opportunity, beckoning investors and entrepreneurs to partake in its growth story."

He reflected on the myriad barriers and obstacles that

hindered trade and investment in Africa, from high tariffs and cumbersome customs procedures to inadequate infrastructure and regulatory constraints. Yet, amidst these challenges, Alex saw a resilience and determination that was uniquely African, a spirit of innovation and entrepreneurship that refused to be subdued.

"Despite the challenges, Africa's potential is boundless," Alex wrote, his voice filled with optimism. "Through collaboration, cooperation, and collective action, African countries can overcome the barriers to trade and investment, unlocking new opportunities for growth, prosperity, and development."

He thought back to the insights and perspectives shared by experts and practitioners throughout his journey, from the importance of regional trade blocs and infrastructure development to the need for policy coordination and institutional reforms. Each conversation had added a layer of understanding, painting a richer picture of Africa's economic landscape and the path forward.

"As I conclude this chapter of my journey, I am filled with hope and excitement for the future of Africa," Alex wrote, his words imbued with a sense of purpose. "Trade and regional integration hold the key to unlocking the continent's vast potential, forging a path towards prosperity and opportunity for all who call Africa home."

With a sense of satisfaction, Alex closed his notebook, knowing that his journey was far from over. As he drifted off to sleep, visions of a vibrant, interconnected Africa danced in his mind, a testament to the boundless possibilities that lay ahead.

13

Chapter 13: Social Impact and Responsible Investing

13.1: The Importance of Social Impact Investing

As the dawn broke over the horizon, casting a golden hue over the cityscape, Alex embarked on a new chapter of his journey—one that delved into the realm of social impact and responsible investing in Africa. Guiding him on this leg of his exploration was Ms. Fatima Kamara, a passionate advocate for social change and responsible business practices.

Ms. Kamara welcomed Alex into her office, a sanctuary adorned with posters, photographs, and inspirational quotes that spoke to the transformative power of social impact investing. "Good morning, Alex," she greeted warmly. "Today, we'll delve into the world of social impact investing, exploring its significance in driving positive change and sustainable development in Africa."

Eager to learn, Alex settled into his seat as Ms. Kamara began to elucidate the intricacies of social impact investing. "Social impact investing is more than just a financial transaction; it's a catalyst for change, empowering investors to generate positive social and environmental outcomes alongside financial returns," she explained. "In Africa, where social and economic challenges abound, social impact investing holds the promise of addressing pressing issues such as poverty, inequality, and environmental degradation."

She highlighted the key features of social impact investing, emphasizing factors such as intentionality, measurability, and accountability. "Social impact investing seeks to deploy capital to enterprises and projects that generate measurable social and environmental impact," Ms. Kamara said. "By aligning financial goals with social and environmental objectives, investors can drive meaningful change and contribute to the achievement of the Sustainable Development Goals."

To provide a tangible example, Ms. Kamara arranged for Alex to visit a social enterprise in Africa, where he witnessed firsthand the transformative power of impact investing in action. He observed entrepreneurs, community leaders, and investors coming together to address local challenges, from access to clean water and sanitation to healthcare and education, a testament to the potential of social impact investing to drive positive change at the grassroots level.

"As African countries seek to achieve inclusive and sustainable development, social impact investing has emerged as a powerful tool for unlocking capital, fostering innovation, and addressing pressing social and environmental challenges," Ms. Kamara explained. "By harnessing the power of finance for good, investors can create shared value for communities, businesses, and the environment, paving the way for a more equitable and sustainable future for all."

As they delved deeper into the discussion, Ms. Kamara emphasized the importance of collaboration, transparency, and stakeholder engagement in advancing social impact investing in Africa. "Efforts to promote social impact investing must be grounded in principles of transparency, accountability, and inclusivity," she said. "By fostering partnerships between investors, governments, civil society, and communities, we can unlock the full potential of social impact investing to drive positive change and transform lives."

Later that afternoon, Ms. Kamara arranged for Alex to attend a symposium on social impact investing in Africa. The symposium brought together investors, entrepreneurs, and social innovators to share best practices, showcase success stories, and explore opportunities for collaboration and partnership in advancing social impact investing on the continent.

Alex found the symposium enlightening, gaining valuable insights into the transformative potential of social impact investing and the role of finance in driving social and environmental change. He was inspired by the dedication of stakeholders to making a difference in their communities and the potential for collaboration and partnership to create lasting impact.

As the symposium came to a close, Alex thanked Ms. Kamara for her insights and hospitality. He left her office feeling inspired and energized, knowing that the knowledge and connections he had gained would be invaluable in understanding the complexities and opportunities of social impact investing in Africa.

Back at his hotel, Alex reflected on the day's discussions. Social impact investing was not just about financial returns; it was about creating positive change, empowering communities, and building a better future for generations to come. Armed with this understanding, he felt ready to explore opportunities in social impact investing, knowing that the insights and connections he had gained would be instrumental in making a difference in Africa and beyond.

13.2: ESG Criteria in Investment Decisions

As the sun reached its zenith, casting a warm glow over the bustling streets below, Alex continued his journey into the realm of social impact and responsible investing in Africa. This leg of his exploration was guided by Mr. Samuel Mbeki, a seasoned investor renowned for his expertise in integrating environmental, social, and governance (ESG) criteria into investment decisions.

Mr. Mbeki welcomed Alex into his office, a space adorned with charts, graphs, and sustainability reports that underscored the importance of ESG considerations in investment management. "Good afternoon, Alex," he greeted warmly. "Today, we'll delve into the world of ESG criteria in investment decisions, exploring their significance in driving sustainable returns and positive impact in Africa."

Eager to learn, Alex settled into his seat as Mr. Mbeki began to elucidate the intricacies of ESG criteria. "ESG criteria are a set of environmental, social, and governance factors that investors consider when evaluating potential investments," he explained. "These criteria provide a framework for assessing the sustainability and ethical impact of investment opportunities, helping investors to manage risks, enhance returns, and contribute to positive social and environmental outcomes."

He highlighted the key components of ESG criteria, emphasizing factors such as climate change mitigation, human rights, labor practices, diversity and inclusion, and corporate governance. "ESG criteria enable investors to identify companies and projects that are aligned with sustainable development goals and values," Mr. Mbeki said. "By integrating ESG considerations into investment decisions, investors can mitigate risks, seize opportunities, and drive positive change in the companies and communities in which they invest."

To provide a tangible example, Mr. Mbeki arranged for Alex to meet with a portfolio manager who specialized in ESG-focused investments in Africa. They discussed how ESG criteria were integrated into the investment process, from screening potential investments for environmental and social risks to engaging with companies on sustainability issues and measuring impact.

"As African countries seek to attract investment and achieve sustainable development, ESG criteria are increasingly becoming a key consideration for investors," Mr. Mbeki explained. "By incorporating ESG considerations into investment decisions, investors can not only enhance financial performance but also contribute to positive social and environmental outcomes, creating shared value for shareholders, stakeholders, and society at large."

As they delved deeper into the discussion, Mr. Mbeki emphasized the importance of transparency, disclosure, and collaboration in advancing ESG integration in Africa. "Efforts to promote ESG integration must be grounded in principles of transparency, accountability, and stakeholder engagement," he said. "By fostering dialogue and collaboration between investors, companies, regulators, and civil society, we can

CHAPTER 13: SOCIAL IMPACT AND RESPONSIBLE INVESTING

unlock the full potential of ESG criteria to drive sustainable development and create value for all stakeholders."

Later that evening, Mr. Mbeki arranged for Alex to attend a conference on sustainable finance and responsible investment in Africa. The conference brought together investors, asset managers, and sustainability experts to discuss best practices, showcase success stories, and explore opportunities for collaboration and partnership in advancing ESG integration on the continent.

Alex found the conference enlightening, gaining valuable insights into the transformative potential of ESG integration and the role of finance in driving sustainable development. He was inspired by the commitment of stakeholders to integrating ESG criteria into investment decisions and the potential for collaboration and partnership to create lasting impact.

As the conference came to a close, Alex thanked Mr. Mbeki for his insights and hospitality. He left his office feeling inspired and energized, knowing that the knowledge and connections he had gained would be invaluable in understanding the complexities and opportunities of ESG integration in Africa.

Back at his hotel, Alex reflected on the day's discussions. ESG criteria were not just about screening investments; they were about creating value, driving positive change, and building a better future for generations to come. Armed with this understanding, he felt ready to explore opportunities in responsible investing, knowing that the insights and connections he had gained would be instrumental in making a difference in Africa and beyond.

3.3: Case Studies of Successful Impact Investments

As the city lights twinkled against the night sky, Alex delved deeper into the world of social impact and responsible investing in Africa. Guiding him on this leg of his journey was Ms. Sarah Ofori, a visionary investor known for her commitment to driving positive change through impactful investments. Together, they embarked on a journey through the stories of real organizations and companies making a difference on the continent.

Their first stop was at SolarNow, a pioneering solar energy company providing clean and affordable energy solutions to off-grid communities across Africa. Alex marveled at the solar panels gleaming under the African sun, a testament to the company's commitment to sustainability and energy access. Ms. Ofori explained how SolarNow's innovative financing model had enabled thousands of households and businesses to access clean energy, improving livelihoods, powering economic growth, and reducing carbon emissions.

Next, they visited Twiga Foods, a technology-driven agricultural supply chain platform revolutionizing the way food is sourced, distributed, and sold in Africa. Alex observed the bustling marketplace, where farmers, traders, and consumers converged to buy and sell fresh produce. Ms. Ofori shared how Twiga Foods leveraged data analytics, mobile technology, and logistics optimization to connect smallholder farmers with markets, reduce food waste, and increase incomes for farmers and traders alike.

Their journey continued to M-KOPA Solar, a leading provider of pay-as-you-go solar home systems and appliances. Alex marveled at the sight of families enjoying the benefits of

CHAPTER 13: SOCIAL IMPACT AND RESPONSIBLE INVESTING

clean, reliable electricity in their homes, thanks to M-KOPA's innovative financing model and distribution network. Ms. Ofori explained how M-KOPA had transformed the lives of millions of off-grid households, providing access to energy, lighting, and entertainment, while also promoting financial inclusion and economic empowerment.

Their final stop was at Jibu, a social enterprise empowering entrepreneurs to own and operate clean water franchises in underserved communities. Alex witnessed the joy on people's faces as they filled their jerry cans with clean, safe drinking water from Jibu's locally-owned and operated water kiosks. Ms. Ofori shared how Jibu's franchise model had created opportunities for entrepreneurship, improved health outcomes, and strengthened communities, all while promoting sustainable water management and conservation.

As they reflected on their journey, Alex and Ms. Ofori were inspired by the stories of impact and innovation they had encountered. From clean energy and agriculture to water and finance, these real-world examples demonstrated the transformative power of impact investing in Africa, driving positive change, creating shared value, and building a brighter future for all.

As they bid farewell to each other, Alex felt a renewed sense of purpose and determination. The stories of SolarNow, Twiga Foods, M-KOPA Solar, and Jibu had opened his eyes to the vast potential of impact investing in Africa, inspiring him to seek out opportunities to drive positive change and make a difference in the world. Armed with newfound knowledge and inspiration, Alex set out to continue his journey, knowing that the path ahead was filled with endless possibilities for impact and innovation.

13.4: Measuring Social and Environmental Impact

As the sun dipped below the horizon, casting a warm glow over the city skyline, Alex delved deeper into the intricacies of social impact and responsible investing in Africa. Guiding him on this leg of his journey was Dr. Jane Omondi, a renowned economist and expert in impact measurement and evaluation. Together, they embarked on a quest to understand how social and environmental impact could be quantified and assessed.

Their first stop was at Impact Hub, a vibrant community of social entrepreneurs and changemakers dedicated to driving positive change through innovative solutions. Alex marveled at the diverse array of projects and initiatives underway, from renewable energy and sustainable agriculture to education and healthcare. Dr. Omondi explained how Impact Hub leveraged a range of tools and methodologies to measure and evaluate the social and environmental impact of its members' ventures, from outcome mapping and theory of change to social return on investment (SROI) analysis.

Next, they visited Acumen, a pioneering impact investment fund focused on tackling poverty and inequality through patient capital and innovative business models. Alex was impressed by Acumen's rigorous approach to impact measurement, which encompassed a holistic assessment of social, environmental, and financial performance. Dr. Omondi shared how Acumen used a combination of qualitative and quantitative metrics, including surveys, interviews, and case studies, to track and evaluate the impact of its investments on target communities and beneficiaries.

Their journey continued to Dalberg, a global consulting firm specializing in social impact strategy and measurement.

CHAPTER 13: SOCIAL IMPACT AND RESPONSIBLE INVESTING

Alex observed the team of analysts and researchers crunching numbers and analyzing data to assess the effectiveness of social programs and interventions. Dr. Omondi explained how Dalberg employed a range of methodologies, including randomized controlled trials, cost-benefit analysis, and impact evaluations, to measure the social and environmental impact of its clients' initiatives and investments.

Their final stop was at the African Institute for Development Policy (AFIDEP), a leading research institute dedicated to evidence-based policymaking and program evaluation. Alex witnessed the team of researchers and experts conducting fieldwork and collecting data to assess the impact of health, education, and governance programs across Africa. Dr. Omondi shared how AFIDEP used a combination of qualitative and quantitative research methods, including surveys, focus group discussions, and policy analysis, to generate insights and recommendations for policymakers and practitioners.

As they reflected on their journey, Alex and Dr. Omondi were struck by the complexity and nuance of impact measurement and evaluation. From Impact Hub and Acumen to Dalberg and AFIDEP, these real-world examples demonstrated the importance of robust methodologies, rigorous analysis, and stakeholder engagement in assessing the social and environmental impact of investments and initiatives in Africa.

As they bid farewell to each other, Alex felt a newfound appreciation for the power of data and evidence in driving social change and environmental stewardship. Inspired by the work of Impact Hub, Acumen, Dalberg, and AFIDEP, he resolved to incorporate impact measurement and evaluation into his own investment practices, knowing that by measuring impact, he could maximize the positive outcomes of his investments and contribute to a more equitable and sustainable future for Africa and beyond.

13.5: Challenges in Impact Investing

As twilight descended upon the city, Alex found himself immersed in the complexities of social impact and responsible investing in Africa. Guiding him through this intricate terrain was Dr. Fatima Abiola, a seasoned practitioner with years of experience navigating the challenges and opportunities of impact investing. Together, they embarked on a journey to uncover the obstacles and hurdles that investors faced in their quest to drive positive change.

Their first destination was a roundtable discussion at the African Development Bank, where policymakers, investors, and development practitioners gathered to address the challenges of impact investing in Africa. Alex listened intently as stakeholders shared their perspectives on issues such as regulatory uncertainty, political instability, and lack of access to finance, which hindered the growth of impact investing on the continent. Dr. Abiola emphasized the importance of creating an enabling environment for impact investment, one that incentivized innovation, promoted transparency, and fostered collaboration between government, private sector, and civil society.

Next, they visited a social enterprise incubator in the heart of the city, where aspiring entrepreneurs grappled with the realities of scaling their ventures and accessing capital. Alex witnessed the passion and determination of these changemakers as they navigated the challenges of market validation, talent acquisition, and financial sustainability. Dr.

Abiola underscored the need for patient capital and tailored support to help early-stage enterprises overcome the hurdles they faced on their journey to scale and impact.

Their journey continued to a rural community on the outskirts of the city, where access to basic services such as healthcare, education, and clean water remained elusive for many. Alex observed the resilience and resourcefulness of community leaders as they sought to address the root causes of poverty and inequality through grassroots initiatives and social enterprises. Dr. Abiola highlighted the importance of community engagement, empowerment, and ownership in driving sustainable development and social change from the bottom up.

Their final stop was at a high-level summit on impact investing, where leaders from across sectors and industries convened to chart a course for the future of impact investing in Africa. Alex was inspired by the commitment and collaboration on display as stakeholders discussed strategies to overcome barriers such as limited data and metrics, fragmented ecosystems, and capacity constraints. Dr. Abiola emphasized the need for collective action and partnership to address these challenges and unlock the full potential of impact investing to drive positive change and sustainable development in Africa.

As they reflected on their journey, Alex and Dr. Abiola were struck by the enormity of the task ahead. From regulatory hurdles and access to finance to capacity building and ecosystem development, the challenges of impact investing in Africa were manifold and complex. Yet, amidst these challenges, they saw opportunities for innovation, collaboration, and transformation, knowing that by working together, they could overcome barriers and create a future where impact investing was not just a choice, but a necessity for building a more equitable and sustainable world for all.

13.6: Summary and Conclusion

As the stars illuminated the night sky, casting a gentle glow over the city, Alex and Dr. Abiola concluded their exploration of social impact and responsible investing in Africa. Sitting beneath the canopy of a towering baobab tree, they reflected on the journey they had undertaken, the lessons they had learned, and the vision they shared for the future of impact investing on the continent.

"Through our journey, we have witnessed the power of impact investing to drive positive change and sustainable development in Africa," Dr. Abiola began, her voice filled with conviction. "From clean energy and agriculture to water and finance, we have seen how investors are leveraging capital, innovation, and collaboration to address pressing social and environmental challenges and create shared value for communities and stakeholders."

Alex nodded in agreement, his gaze fixed on the twinkling stars above. "Indeed, impact investing holds the promise of unlocking new opportunities, mobilizing resources, and catalyzing innovation to build a more equitable and sustainable future for Africa," he added, his voice filled with optimism.

Dr. Abiola continued, "Yet, as we have seen, the path to impact investing is not without its challenges. From regulatory barriers and access to finance to capacity constraints and ecosystem development, there are hurdles to overcome and obstacles to navigate. But amidst these challenges, there is hope."

Alex nodded in understanding, his heart filled with determination. "By working together, we can overcome these challenges and unlock the full potential of impact investing to drive positive change and create a brighter future for Africa and beyond," he affirmed.

As they sat beneath the baobab tree, surrounded by the sounds of the night, Alex and Dr. Abiola shared a moment of silence, a moment of reflection, a moment of gratitude for the journey they had shared and the insights they had gained.

As dawn broke on the horizon, casting a golden glow over the landscape, Alex and Dr. Abiola rose from their seats, ready to embark on the next chapter of their journey—together, they would continue to champion the cause of social impact and responsible investing, knowing that by working together, they could make a difference, one investment at a time.

14

Chapter 14: Case Studies of Successful Investments

14.1: Case Study: Technology Startups

As the sun rose over the city skyline, illuminating the bustling streets below, Alex delved into the world of successful investments in Africa. Guiding him on this leg of his journey was Mr. David Njoroge, a seasoned investor renowned for his success in backing technology startups across the continent. Together, they embarked on a journey to explore the stories of innovation, resilience, and success that characterized Africa's thriving tech ecosystem.

Their first stop was at Andela, a pioneering technology company that was revolutionizing the way Africa's top talent was trained, hired, and deployed to global companies. Alex marveled at the bustling office space, where software engineers and developers collaborated on projects for leading tech firms around the world. Mr. Njoroge shared how Andela had attracted investment from top Silicon Valley investors, positioning itself as a leader in Africa's burgeoning tech industry.

Next, they visited Flutterwave, a fintech startup that was transforming the way Africans transacted and did business online. Alex observed the team of engineers and designers working tirelessly to build innovative payment solutions that catered to the unique needs and challenges of the African market. Mr. Njoroge explained how Flutterwave had raised significant funding from both local and international investors, enabling it to expand its operations across the continent and beyond.

Their journey continued to Cellulant, a leading mobile commerce company that was driving financial inclusion and digital empowerment across Africa. Alex witnessed the impact of Cellulant's mobile payment solutions, which enabled millions of Africans to access financial services, make payments, and conduct business on their mobile phones. Mr. Njoroge highlighted how Cellulant had attracted investment from global giants such as the International Finance Corporation (IFC), signaling its potential to become a key player in Africa's digital economy.

Their final stop was at Jumia, Africa's largest e-commerce platform, which had recently made history with its landmark initial public offering (IPO) on the New York Stock Exchange. Alex marveled at the scale and scope of Jumia's operations, which spanned multiple countries and served millions of customers across the continent. Mr. Njoroge shared how Jumia's success had attracted investment from top-tier investors, validating Africa's potential as a lucrative market for e-commerce and technology.

As they reflected on their journey, Alex and Mr. Njoroge

were struck by the resilience, innovation, and success that characterized Africa's technology startups. From Andela and Flutterwave to Cellulant and Jumia, these real-world examples demonstrated the transformative power of technology to drive economic growth, create jobs, and improve livelihoods across the continent.

As they bid farewell to each other, Alex felt inspired and energized, knowing that the stories of Andela, Flutterwave, Cellulant, and Jumia were just the beginning of Africa's journey towards becoming a global hub for technology and innovation. Armed with newfound knowledge and inspiration, he set out to explore opportunities to invest in Africa's vibrant tech ecosystem, knowing that by backing the next generation of innovators and entrepreneurs, he could contribute to the continent's continued growth and prosperity.

14.3: Case Study: Agribusiness Ventures

As the morning sun bathed the countryside in golden light, Alex embarked on a journey to uncover the success stories of agribusiness ventures in Africa. Joining him on this expedition was Ms. Aisha Ibrahim, a seasoned investor with a passion for agriculture and sustainable development. Together, they set out to explore the transformative impact of investments in Africa's agricultural sector.

Their first destination was Zambeef, a leading agribusiness company that was revolutionizing the way food was produced, processed, and distributed in Zambia. Alex marveled at the sprawling farms and processing facilities, where teams of farmers and workers labored tirelessly to produce high-quality meat and dairy products. Ms. Ibrahim shared how Zambeef had leveraged investment capital to modernize its operations, improve productivity, and expand its market reach, becoming a key player in Zambia's agricultural value chain.

Next, they visited Twiga Foods, a technology-driven agricultural supply chain platform that was connecting smallholder farmers with markets in Kenya. Alex observed the bustling marketplace, where farmers sold their produce directly to buyers using Twiga's mobile app. Ms. Ibrahim explained how Twiga had attracted investment from both local and international investors, enabling it to scale its operations, increase farmer incomes, and reduce food waste through efficient logistics and distribution.

Their journey continued to Sunculture, a solar-powered irrigation company that was empowering farmers across Africa to harness the power of the sun to grow crops and improve livelihoods. Alex witnessed the installation of solar-powered irrigation systems, which enabled farmers to access water for irrigation year-round, increasing crop yields and incomes. Ms. Ibrahim highlighted how Sunculture had attracted investment from impact investors and venture capital firms, positioning itself as a leader in sustainable agriculture and climate-smart farming practices.

Their final stop was at Olam International, a global agribusiness company that was investing in Africa's agricultural value chains from farm to fork. Alex marveled at the diversity of Olam's operations, which spanned multiple countries and commodities, from cocoa and coffee to grains and spices. Ms. Ibrahim shared how Olam had partnered with farmers, governments, and communities to promote sustainable agriculture, enhance food security, and create shared value for all stakeholders.

As they reflected on their journey, Alex and Ms. Ibrahim were struck by the resilience, innovation, and impact that characterized Africa's agribusiness ventures. From Zambeef and Twiga Foods to Sunculture and Olam International, these real-world examples demonstrated the transformative power of investments in agriculture to drive economic growth, create jobs, and improve livelihoods across the continent.

As they bid farewell to each other, Alex felt inspired and invigorated, knowing that the stories of Zambeef, Twiga Foods, Sunculture, and Olam International were just the beginning of Africa's journey towards agricultural transformation. Armed with newfound knowledge and inspiration, he set out to explore opportunities to invest in Africa's vibrant agribusiness sector, knowing that by backing innovative and sustainable ventures, he could contribute to the continent's continued prosperity and development.

14.4: Case Study: Real Estate Development

As the sun reached its zenith, casting a warm glow over the urban landscape, Alex embarked on a journey to explore the success stories of real estate development in Africa. Joining him on this venture was Mr. Kwame Mensah, a seasoned real estate investor with a keen eye for opportunity and innovation. Together, they set out to uncover the transformative impact of investments in Africa's dynamic real estate sector.

Their first destination was The Pearls of Africa, a landmark mixed-use development project that was reshaping the skyline of Kampala, Uganda. Alex marveled at the towering skyscrapers, luxury residences, and state-of-the-art commercial spaces that comprised The Pearls, a testament to the vision and ambition of its developers. Mr. Mensah shared how The Pearls had attracted investment from local and international investors, positioning itself as a premier destination for living, working, and leisure in East Africa.

Next, they visited Eko Atlantic City, a groundbreaking urban development project that was reclaiming land from the Atlantic Ocean to create a new city on the coast of Lagos, Nigeria. Alex observed the construction of roads, bridges, and infrastructure, which would soon connect Eko Atlantic City to the heart of Lagos. Mr. Mensah explained how Eko Atlantic had attracted investment from sovereign wealth funds and institutional investors, transforming a vision of resilience and sustainability into a reality.

Their journey continued to Kigali Heights, a mixed-use development project that was elevating the urban landscape of Kigali, Rwanda. Alex marveled at the sleek architecture, vibrant retail spaces, and upscale offices that comprised Kigali Heights, a symbol of Rwanda's economic transformation and urban renewal. Mr. Mensah highlighted how Kigali Heights had attracted investment from local entrepreneurs and international developers, catalyzing economic growth and creating employment opportunities in the heart of Rwanda's capital.

Their final stop was at Victoria Island, a prime waterfront district in Lagos, Nigeria, that was undergoing a renaissance of investment and development. Alex witnessed the construction of luxury condominiums, waterfront promenades, and world-class amenities that were transforming Victoria Island into a premier destination for living, working, and recreation. Mr. Mensah shared how Victoria Island had attracted investment from high-net-worth individuals and multinational corporations, fueling the city's growth and prosperity.

As they reflected on their journey, Alex and Mr. Mensah were struck by the scale, scope, and impact of real estate development in Africa. From The Pearls of Africa and Eko Atlantic City to Kigali Heights and Victoria Island, these real-world examples demonstrated the transformative power of investments in real estate to drive economic growth, create jobs, and improve quality of life across the continent.

As they bid farewell to each other, Alex felt inspired and energized, knowing that the stories of The Pearls of Africa, Eko Atlantic City, Kigali Heights, and Victoria Island were just the beginning of Africa's journey towards urban development and prosperity. Armed with newfound knowledge and inspiration, he set out to explore opportunities to invest in Africa's dynamic real estate sector, knowing that by backing innovative and sustainable projects, he could contribute to the continent's continued growth and development.

14.5: Lessons Learned from Failures

As the sun began to dip below the horizon, casting long shadows across the city streets, Alex and Mr. Mensah sat down to reflect on the lessons learned from failures in the world of investments. With a somber tone, they embarked on a journey to uncover the valuable insights that could be gleaned from setbacks and disappointments.

Their first tale took them to a once-promising agricultural venture in Ghana, where ambitious plans to cultivate cash crops for export had fallen short due to unforeseen challenges such as drought, pest infestations, and market volatility. Alex listened intently as Mr. Mensah recounted the importance of conducting thorough due diligence, assessing risk factors, and building resilience into investment strategies to mitigate potential losses.

Next, they explored the story of a real estate development project in Kenya, where delays in regulatory approvals, cost overruns, and legal disputes had derailed plans to build a luxury resort on the coast. Alex nodded in understanding as Mr. Mensah emphasized the importance of managing expectations, establishing clear timelines, and fostering open communication with stakeholders to navigate complex projects and avoid costly pitfalls.

Their journey continued to a technology startup in Nigeria, where high expectations and lofty ambitions had collided with harsh realities such as fierce competition, changing market dynamics, and internal mismanagement. Alex reflected on the need for entrepreneurs and investors alike to stay agile, adaptive, and responsive to shifting trends and customer preferences in order to remain relevant and sustainable in a rapidly evolving landscape.

Their final stop was at a renewable energy project in South Africa, where ambitious plans to harness solar power for rural electrification had been hampered by technical challenges, funding constraints, and regulatory hurdles. Alex pondered the importance of aligning investment objectives with local needs and priorities, engaging with communities and stakeholders, and building partnerships to leverage expertise and resources for maximum impact.

As they reflected on their journey, Alex and Mr. Mensah were struck by the resilience, determination, and wisdom that could be gained from setbacks and failures. From agricultural ventures and real estate developments to technology startups and renewable energy projects, these cautionary tales served as valuable reminders of the inherent risks and uncertainties of investing in Africa, but also the potential for growth, innovation, and impact when approached with humility, perseverance, and a willingness to learn.

As they bid farewell to each other, Alex felt a newfound appreciation for the lessons learned from failures, knowing that by embracing setbacks and challenges as opportunities for growth and reflection, he could become a wiser and more resilient investor, capable of navigating the complexities of the African investment landscape with confidence and conviction.

14.6: Summary and Conclusion

Under the canopy of a starlit sky, Alex and Mr. Mensah concluded their exploration of case studies in successful investments, reflecting on the diverse stories of triumph, resilience, and innovation they had encountered along their journey.

"As we've seen through our exploration of various investment ventures," Mr. Mensah began, his voice resonating with wisdom, "success in Africa is not just about financial returns, but about creating lasting impact, driving positive change, and fostering sustainable development across the continent."

Alex nodded in agreement, his mind still buzzing with the myriad experiences they had encountered. "Indeed," he replied, "whether it's technology startups, agribusiness ventures, or real estate developments, the common thread that binds these success stories is the vision, passion, and commitment of the people behind them."

Mr. Mensah continued, "Yet, as we've also learned, success

rarely comes without its share of challenges and setbacks. From regulatory hurdles and market volatility to technical challenges and funding constraints, the path to success is often fraught with obstacles that require resilience, perseverance, and adaptability to overcome."

Alex nodded in understanding, reflecting on the lessons learned from failures and setbacks. "But amidst these challenges," he remarked, "there are also opportunities for growth, innovation, and transformation. By embracing setbacks as opportunities for learning and growth, we can become wiser, more resilient investors capable of navigating the complexities of the African investment landscape with confidence and conviction."

As they sat beneath the starlit sky, surrounded by the quiet beauty of the night, Alex and Mr. Mensah shared a moment of reflection, gratitude, and hope for the future of investment in Africa. With a renewed sense of purpose and determination, they bid farewell to each other, knowing that the stories of success and resilience they had encountered were just the beginning of Africa's journey towards prosperity and development.

Armed with newfound knowledge, inspiration, and a deep appreciation for the transformative power of investment, they set out to continue their respective journeys, knowing that by investing in Africa's people, ideas, and potential, they could contribute to a brighter, more prosperous future for all.

15

Chapter 15: Future Prospects and Strategies for Investors

15.1: Emerging Trends in African Markets

As dawn painted the horizon in shades of pink and gold, Alex and Ms. Ibrahim delved into the future prospects and strategies for investors in African markets. With a sense of anticipation, they embarked on a journey to explore the emerging trends shaping the continent's investment landscape.

Their first stop was at the intersection of technology and finance, where they witnessed the rise of fintech startups and digital payment platforms revolutionizing access to financial services and driving financial inclusion across Africa. Alex marveled at the proliferation of mobile money and digital banking solutions, which were empowering millions of Africans to save, borrow, and invest in ways previously unimaginable.

Next, they ventured into the realm of renewable energy and

sustainable development, where they observed the growing momentum behind clean energy projects and climate-smart initiatives aimed at addressing Africa's energy challenges while mitigating the impacts of climate change. Ms. Ibrahim shared how investments in solar, wind, and hydro power were unlocking new opportunities for growth, innovation, and resilience across the continent.

Their journey continued to the agricultural sector, where they witnessed the increasing importance of value-added processing, mechanization, and agribusiness ventures in driving agricultural transformation and food security in Africa. Alex marveled at the potential for investments in smart farming technologies, supply chain innovations, and market linkages to unlock new opportunities for farmers and entrepreneurs alike.

Their final stop was at the nexus of infrastructure and urban development, where they observed the rapid pace of urbanization and the need for sustainable, inclusive urban planning solutions to accommodate Africa's growing population and unlock its economic potential. Ms. Ibrahim highlighted how investments in transportation networks, affordable housing, and smart cities were reshaping the urban landscape and creating new opportunities for investment and growth.

As they reflected on their journey, Alex and Ms. Ibrahim were struck by the dynamic nature of African markets and the wealth of opportunities they presented for investors willing to embrace change, innovation, and uncertainty. From fintech and renewable energy to agriculture and urban development, the emerging trends shaping Africa's investment landscape offered a glimpse into the continent's boundless potential for growth and development.

As they bid farewell to each other, Alex felt a sense of excitement and optimism for the future of investment in Africa, knowing that by staying informed, adaptable, and forward-thinking, he could position himself to capitalize on the emerging trends and opportunities shaping the continent's future. Armed with newfound knowledge and inspiration, he set out to continue his journey as an investor in Africa, knowing that the best was yet to come.

15.2: Strategies for Long-term Investment

As the sun climbed higher in the sky, Alex and Ms. Ibrahim delved into the strategies for long-term investment in African markets, recognizing the importance of patience, foresight, and resilience in navigating the complexities of the investment landscape.

Their first strategy was diversification, as they discussed the importance of spreading investment across different asset classes, sectors, and geographic regions to minimize risk and maximize returns. Alex nodded in agreement, understanding the need to balance high-risk, high-reward opportunities with more stable, income-generating assets to achieve a well-rounded investment portfolio.

Next, they explored the value of strategic partnerships and alliances, emphasizing the importance of collaborating with local partners, communities, and stakeholders to gain insights, access resources, and mitigate risks in unfamiliar markets. Ms. Ibrahim shared examples of successful partnerships that had enabled investors to leverage local knowledge, networks, and expertise to navigate regulatory hurdles, cultural nuances, and market dynamics more effectively.

Their discussion then turned to the importance of due diligence and research, as they highlighted the need for investors to conduct thorough analysis, assess risk factors, and gather reliable data to inform investment decisions. Alex reflected on the lessons learned from their journey, recognizing the value of staying informed, adaptable, and open-minded in the face of uncertainty and complexity.

Their final strategy was patience and resilience, as they emphasized the importance of taking a long-term view and maintaining a steady course in the face of market fluctuations, economic downturns, and unforeseen challenges. Ms. Ibrahim shared stories of successful investors who had weathered storms, overcome setbacks, and ultimately reaped the rewards of their perseverance, determination, and faith in Africa's potential for growth and development.

As they concluded their discussion, Alex and Ms. Ibrahim felt a renewed sense of purpose and confidence in their ability to navigate the complexities of African markets and seize the opportunities that lay ahead. Armed with a clear vision, sound strategies, and a commitment to long-term investment, they set out to continue their journey as investors in Africa, knowing that by staying true to their principles and values, they could contribute to the continent's continued prosperity and development.

15.3: The Role of Innovation in Future Investments

As the day progressed, Alex and Ms. Ibrahim explored the role of innovation in shaping future investments in African markets, recognizing the transformative power of technology, creativity, and ingenuity in driving economic growth and development.

Their discussion began with a focus on technological innovation, as they marveled at the rapid advancements in fintech, agritech, and renewable energy that were revolutionizing traditional industries and unlocking new opportunities for investment. Alex nodded in agreement, recognizing the potential for disruptive technologies to address key challenges such as financial inclusion, food security, and energy access in Africa.

Next, they explored the importance of social and environmental innovation, as they discussed the growing emphasis on sustainability, impact investing, and corporate social responsibility in shaping investment decisions and driving positive change in communities and ecosystems across the continent. Ms. Ibrahim shared examples of companies and organizations that were leveraging innovation to create shared value, foster social inclusion, and protect the environment while generating financial returns for investors.

Their discussion then turned to the role of entrepreneurship and startup culture in fueling innovation and driving economic growth in Africa. Alex reflected on the vibrant ecosystem of tech hubs, incubators, and accelerators that were nurturing the next generation of African entrepreneurs and innovators, empowering them to turn bold ideas into scalable businesses that addressed local challenges and global markets.

Their final topic of discussion was the importance of regulatory innovation, as they explored the role of governments and policymakers in creating an enabling environment for innovation, entrepreneurship, and investment in Africa. Ms. Ibrahim emphasized the need for regulatory frameworks that balanced innovation with consumer protection, market stability, and ethical considerations, fostering a culture of innovation that was inclusive, responsible, and sustainable.

As they concluded their discussion, Alex and Ms. Ibrahim felt inspired by the potential of innovation to drive positive change and unlock new opportunities for investment in Africa. Armed with a deeper understanding of the role of innovation in shaping future investments, they set out to continue their journey as forward-thinking investors, knowing that by embracing innovation and creativity, they could contribute to a brighter, more prosperous future for Africa and its people.

15.4: Leveraging Local Partnerships

As the sun began to set, casting a warm glow over the landscape, Alex and Ms. Ibrahim delved into the importance of leveraging local partnerships in shaping future investments in African markets. Recognizing the value of local knowledge, networks, and expertise, they embarked on a discussion to explore the transformative potential of collaboration and cooperation with local stakeholders.

Their conversation began with a focus on building trust and relationships, as they emphasized the importance of establishing genuine connections and fostering mutual respect and understanding with local partners. Alex nodded in agreement, recognizing the need to listen, learn, and engage with communities and stakeholders to gain insights, build trust, and cultivate shared goals and aspirations.

Next, they explored the value of local partnerships in navigating regulatory hurdles, cultural nuances, and market dynamics in unfamiliar territories. Ms. Ibrahim shared examples of successful partnerships that had enabled investors to access valuable insights, resources, and opportunities, while also fostering economic empowerment, social inclusion, and sustainable development in local communities.

Their discussion then turned to the importance of capacity-building and skills transfer, as they highlighted the need for investors to invest in training, education, and mentorship programs that empowered local entrepreneurs, businesses, and organizations to thrive and succeed in a rapidly changing world. Alex reflected on the importance of investing in human capital and empowering local talent to drive innovation, entrepreneurship, and economic growth in Africa.

Their final topic of discussion was the role of inclusive and equitable partnerships in fostering resilience and sustainability in African markets. Ms. Ibrahim emphasized the need for partnerships that prioritized social impact, environmental stewardship, and shared value creation, ensuring that investments contributed to the well-being and prosperity of all stakeholders, both now and in the future.

As they concluded their discussion, Alex and Ms. Ibrahim felt inspired by the potential of leveraging local partnerships to drive positive change and unlock new opportunities for investment in Africa. Armed with a deeper understanding of the importance of collaboration, cooperation, and inclusivity, they set out to continue their journey as responsible investors, knowing that by working together with local partners, they could contribute to a brighter, more prosperous future for Africa and its people.

15.5: Policy Recommendations for Governments

As twilight descended upon the horizon, Alex and Ms. Ibrahim delved into the critical role of policy recommendations for governments in shaping future investments in African markets. Recognizing the symbiotic relationship between private sector initiatives and government policies, they embarked on a discussion to explore the key areas where policymakers could play a proactive role in fostering a conducive environment for investment and growth.

Their conversation began with a focus on regulatory reform, as they emphasized the importance of streamlining bureaucratic processes, reducing red tape, and promoting transparency and accountability in regulatory frameworks. Alex nodded in agreement, recognizing the need for clear and consistent regulations that provided certainty and confidence to investors while also safeguarding the interests of consumers and the public.

Next, they explored the importance of infrastructure development, as they highlighted the critical role of governments in investing in essential infrastructure such as transportation networks, energy systems, and digital connectivity to unlock economic potential, enhance competitiveness, and improve quality of life for citizens. Ms. Ibrahim shared examples of successful infrastructure projects that had catalyzed economic growth and development, creating new opportunities for investment and innovation in Africa.

Their discussion then turned to the importance of fostering an enabling environment for entrepreneurship and innovation, as they emphasized the need for governments to invest in education, training, and research and development initiatives that nurtured talent, fostered creativity, and encouraged entrepreneurship among the youth. Alex reflected on the importance of building a culture of innovation and risk-taking that empowered individuals and businesses to pursue bold ideas and ambitious ventures in pursuit of economic growth and prosperity.

Their final topic of discussion was the importance of sustainable and inclusive development, as they explored the role of governments in promoting social equity, environmental stewardship, and shared prosperity through policies that prioritized job creation, social protection, and environmental conservation. Ms. Ibrahim emphasized the need for policies that balanced economic growth with social and environmental considerations, ensuring that investments contributed to the well-being and resilience of communities and ecosystems across the continent.

As they concluded their discussion, Alex and Ms. Ibrahim felt a renewed sense of optimism and determination for the future of investment in Africa, knowing that by working together with governments and policymakers to implement sound policies and regulations, they could create an environment that fostered innovation, entrepreneurship, and sustainable development for generations to come. Armed with a deeper understanding of the importance of policy recommendations for governments, they set out to continue their journey as advocates for positive change and responsible investment in Africa, knowing that by working together with governments and stakeholders, they could contribute to a brighter, more prosperous future for Africa and its people.

15.6: Summary and Conclusion

As the stars began to twinkle in the night sky, Alex and Ms. Ibrahim concluded their exploration of future prospects and strategies for investors in African markets with a sense of satisfaction and purpose. With the lessons learned, insights gained, and aspirations kindled, they embarked on a final reflection to summarize their journey and draw meaningful conclusions.

"In our journey through the landscape of African investments," Ms. Ibrahim began, her voice resonating with wisdom, "we have witnessed the untapped potential, the boundless opportunities, and the transformative power of investments in shaping the future of the continent."

Alex nodded in agreement, his mind filled with the diverse stories, experiences, and insights they had encountered along the way. "Indeed," he replied, "from technology startups and renewable energy projects to agriculture ventures and infrastructure developments, the possibilities for growth, innovation, and impact are limitless."

Ms. Ibrahim continued, "Yet, amidst the promise and potential, we have also encountered challenges and obstacles that require resilience, perseverance, and collaboration to overcome. From regulatory hurdles and market volatility to social inequalities and environmental degradation, the path to success in African markets is not without its share of uncertainties and complexities."

Alex reflected on the importance of staying informed, adaptable, and forward-thinking in the face of change and uncertainty. "But," he remarked, "with the right strategies, partnerships, and policies in place, we can unlock the full potential of African markets and create a future that is inclusive, sustainable, and prosperous for all."

As they gazed up at the starlit sky, Alex and Ms. Ibrahim felt a sense of hope and optimism for the future of investment in Africa. Armed with a deeper understanding of the challenges and opportunities that lay ahead, they set out to continue their journey as investors, advocates, and champions of positive change, knowing that by working together with governments, businesses, and communities, they could contribute to a brighter, more prosperous future for Africa and its people.

With a final exchange of gratitude and camaraderie, they bid farewell to each other, knowing that their journey was just beginning, and that the best was yet to come.

About the Author

Goodson Mumba is a multifaceted individual known for his diverse expertise and prolific contributions across various fields. As an infopreneur, Management Consultant, thought leader, and spiritual leader, he has inspired countless individuals through his insightful teachings and impactful writings. Mumba is also an accomplished author, with several notable works to his name, including "Understanding Corporate Worship," "The Years I Spent in a Week," "Management By Harmony," "The CEO's Diary," "Change to Change" and "Creative Thinking for results" His literary works span topics ranging from business management to personal development and spirituality, reflecting his broad range of interests and insights.

With a Master of Business Leadership (MBL) and a Bachelor of Arts in Theology (BTh), Mumba brings a unique blend of business acumen and spiritual wisdom to his work. His educational background is further enriched by a Group Diploma in Management Studies, providing him with a solid foundation in organizational dynamics and leadership principles. Additionally, Mumba holds diplomas in Education Psychology, Leadership and Management Styles, Organizational Behaviour, Financial Accounting, Economic Growth and Development, and Project Management, showcasing his commitment to continuous learning and professional development.

Mumba's expertise extends beyond traditional academic disciplines, encompassing areas such as Neuro-Linguistic Programming (NLP) and Positive Psychology. His diverse skill set is complemented by a range of certifications, including Creative Problem Solving and Decision Making, Life Coaching Fundamentals and Techniques, Professional Life Coaching, and Performance Management System Design. These certifications reflect Mumba's dedication to equipping himself with the tools and knowledge necessary to empower others and drive positive change.

As an author, Mumba's writings reflect his deep understanding of human nature, organizational dynamics, and spiritual principles. His works offer practical insights, actionable strategies, and inspirational guidance for individuals seeking personal growth, professional success, and spiritual fulfillment. Mumba's holistic approach to life and leadership resonates with readers worldwide, making him a respected figure in both the business and spiritual communities.

Overall, Goodson Mumba's diverse background, extensive knowledge, and profound insights make him a sought-after speaker, mentor, and author. His commitment to excellence, lifelong learning, and service to others continues to inspire individuals to unlock their full potential and lead lives of purpose and significance.

Goodson Mumba is renowned for initiating the concept of Management by Harmony, revolutionizing traditional management practices with a focus on balanced and holistic approaches. He has authored two influential books on this subject: "Introduction to Management by Harmony" and its sequel, "Management by Harmony."

Mumba's work has significantly impacted the field, offering innovative strategies for fostering organizational harmony and efficiency. His contributions continue to shape contemporary management theories and practices.

www.ingramcontent.com/pod-product-compliance
Lightning Source LLC
Chambersburg PA
CBHW071827210526
45479CB00001B/20